Old-House

Dictionary

Old-House Dictionary

AN ILLUSTRATED GUIDE
TO AMERICAN
DOMESTIC ARCHITECTURE
(1600 - 1940)

Written and Illustrated by
Steven J. Phillips

The Preservation Press
National Trust for Historic Preservation

This book is dedicated to Dr. Roderick Sprague and to my parents, Robert and Shirley Phillips.

The Preservation Press
National Trust for Historic Preservation
1785 Massachusetts Avenue, N.W.
Washington, D.C. 20036

The National Trust for Historic Preservation is the only private, non-profit national organization chartered by Congress to encourage public participation in the preservation of sites, buildings, and objects significant in American history and culture. Support is provided by membership dues, endowment funds, contributions, and grants from federal agencies, including the U.S. Department of the Interior, under provisions of the National Historic Preservation Act of 1966. The opinions expressed herein do not necessarily reflect the views or policies of the Interior Department. For information about membership in the National Trust, write to Membership at the above address.

Printed in the United States of America

96 95 94   5 4 3 2

Library of Congress Cataloging in Publication Data

Phillips, Steven J.
    Old-house dictionary: an illustrated guide to American domestic architecture (1600-1940)/written and illustrated by Steven J. Phillips.
        p.   cm.
    Originally published: Lakewood, Colo.: American Source Books, c 1989.
    Includes bibliographical references and index.
    ISBN 0-89133-171-9
    1. Architecture, Domestic--United States--Dictionaries.
    I. Title.
    [NA7205.P48 1992]
    728'.0973--dc20   92-14046

Cover design by Keri Schneider and Steven Phillips

Contents

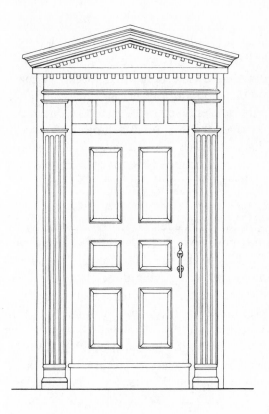

Acknowledgments

Although authors are quite willing to take full responsibility for their creations, they inevitably owe a debt of gratitude to many others. Topping my list are the many dedicated and enthusiastic librarians I have relied on over the life of this project. A special thanks to Mary Ison, Reference Librarian for the Architecture, Design, and Engineering Collections at the Library of Congress.

The earliest stages of this book were by far the most trying. Rick Sprague, Burt Mc-Croskey and Frank Leonhardy helped immeasurably by giving direction to my early research efforts. Additional help was amply provided by E.B., Jane, and Anne Hall, Bob Webber, and Mike Packard. During the last nine months the emphasis shifted from research and drawing to editing, book design, and production. Wayne Bye, Lee Rice, and Judy Richmeier have selflessly given technical and moral support during this final sprint.

Others that deserve special mention include: Tom and Marilyn Ross, Diane Maddex, Dora Crouch, Cort Young, Tom Callaway, Don Palmer, and Jack Stiverson. Thank you for your varied and valued contributions.

Steven J. Phillips
Denver, Colorado

Introduction

Every old house exhibits a unique personality; a personality molded by its designer, its builders, and its occupants. To fully appreciate this uniqueness it is necessary to understand the language of architecture. Dictionaries are the primary means of crossing this language barrier.

Is the ***Old-House Dictionary*** the best architectural dictionary in print? Probably not, but it does have a number of features that set it apart from the others: it is well illustrated, it is easy to understand, it contains cross references and an index, and it deals exclusively with American domestic architecture. These features are briefly discussed below:

- **VISUAL ORIENTATION**

Have you ever had to describe something to someone and ended up saying, "Here, let me draw you a picture"? That's the whole idea behind this book. Instead of using a whole lot of technical terms to describe something, this dictionary uses a whole lot of pictures, and that's much easier for most people to comprehend.

- **CROSS REFERENCES**

So you don't want to thumb through the whole book to find the name of that thing on the roof of an old house that looks like a ceramic pot. Look in the **Roof Cross Reference** to decrease the number of terms you have to search. There are 17 such cross references included at the back of the book.

- **SIMPLE DEFINITIONS**

The job of finding and understanding an unfamiliar architectural term is often no easy task. The goal of this dictionary is to get you, the reader, quickly to the term you are looking for and, once there, provide you with a simple, easily understandable definition. And because the language of architecture is full of jargon, every attempt has been made to clarify possibly confusing words on the spot, or define them elsewhere in the text.

- **INDEX**

Why does this dictionary contain an index? The most obvious answer is that it is one means of getting to a definition when you know the name of the term. But there's another good reason for having an index. Let's say, for example, that you want to make certain that the thin strip of wood attached to a girder is called a *bearer*. Unfortunately, this architectural element is defined under the heading *ledger strip*, which means that you are in for a bit of a search without the aid of an index.

- **QUICK DATA RETRIEVAL**

One hallmark of any good reference work is how quickly it allows the reader to retrieve the desired information. This dictionary has a number of methods for quick data retrieval: the cross references, the index, and the illustrations. But of equal importantance is the page layout. Each page heading in the *Old-House Dictionary* includes the page number and the range of terms found on that page, right up top where the eye naturally goes.

- **GROUPING OF TERMS**

If it's a rafter you're after, you don't have to go to seven places in the dictionary to read about the seven types that are defined; they are all listed under the heading **rafters**. Grouping of related terms saves wear and tear on the book (and probably on your nerves).

- **UN-COMPREHENSIVE**

That's right, un-comprehensive. You won't find the term *chatri* in this dictionary because Hindu architecture isn't covered. Nor will you find *apse*. (Church architecture isn't covered either.) What you will find are terms relating to older American homes that are regional or national in their occurrence. Un-comprehensive is good. Why? Because it cleans out the clutter.

To many of us, old homes represent something very special: maybe a reminder of a time when life was somehow simpler and more predictable, or a living testament to American ingenuity and craftsmanship, or simply a source of personal pride. So whether you're the proud owner of a 1940 bungalow or a professional preservationist, it is hoped that the *Old-House Dictionary* enhances your enjoyment and appreciation of old homes everywhere.

Now, on to the subject at hand: the language of domestic architecture translated through words and illustrations.

Terms
and
Definitions

abacus
The uppermost member of the capital; may be either plain or decorated.

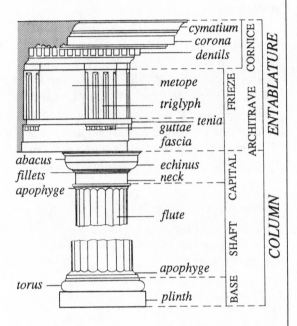

The divisions and elements of a classical order

abutment
A masonry mass used to counteract the thrust of an arch or vault.

acanthus
A plant of the Mediterranean region characterized by thick, fleshy, scalloped leaves; used as a decorative element on Corinthian and composite capitals as well as on moldings.

acanthus

accessories
Parts of ornaments that are not essential to the use and character of a building.

adobes
Unfired, sun-dried mud bricks that are laid up in courses with mud mortar and covered with a protective coating; used as a building material in areas with little rainfall, such as the Southwest. More recent examples contain stabilizers such as portland cement or asphalt, whereas older examples may contain no stabilizers or organic materials (such as straw).
Synonyms: **brick adobes, adobe bricks**

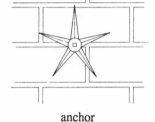

anchor

alcove
A small recessed space that opens into another larger room; an ornamental seat in a garden, a **bower**.

anchor
A metal clamp that helps prevent walls from bulging; often ornamental in appearance.
Synonyms: **tie plate, wall anchor**

anchor bolts
The long bolts that project from the top of the foundation wall and to which the sill of a wood frame structure is secured.

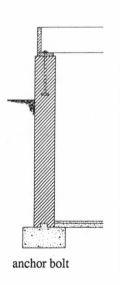

anchor bolt

ante-chamber
An outer chamber or room where guests wait until met by the owner of the house.
Synonyms: **anti-chamber**

anteroom
An outer room that leads to another, more important, room; often used as a waiting room.

anthemion
An ornamental design element based on the palmette or honeysuckle.
Synonyms: **honeysuckle ornament**

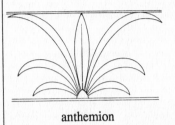
anthemion

apophyge
The slight curve or molding at the top and bottom of the column where the shaft springs from the capital or base. See illustration on page 15.

apron
An either plain or decorated piece of interior trim found directly below the stool of a window. Apron sometimes is used to describe any paneling found on the exterior of a building.

apron

Arabesque
An elaborate design element incorporating geometrical patterns, flowing lines, interwoven flowers, etc.
Synonyms: **Moresque**

arcade
A series of arches supported by columns or pillars; a covered passageway.

arch
A curved and sometimes pointed structural member used to span an opening. Arches are

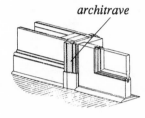

architrave

usually classified either according to historical criteria (e.g., *Tudor* arch, *Moorish* arch, *Gothic* arch) or according to the curve of the underside of the arch. The latter method of classification is the one used in this book.

architrave
In classical architecture and its derivatives, the lowest of the three main parts of the entablature. See illustration on page 15. Also, the ornamental moldings around doors, windows, or other openings.

archivolt
The ornamental band of moldings on the face of an arch.

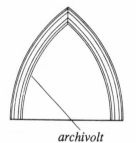

archivolt

areaway
A sunken area around a basement window or doorway; used for access to a basement or cellar, or as a means of admitting light and fresh air for ventilation.

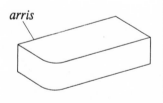

arris

arris
The sharp edge of a brick; the edge where two surfaces meet.

Art Deco (1920 - 1940)
An architectural style characterized by: an overall linear, angular, vertical appearance; stepped facade; extensive use of zig-zags, chevrons, lozenges, and volutes as decorative elements; and vertical projections above the roof line.

Art Moderne (1930 - 1945)

An architectural style characterized by: an overall streamlined appearance, asymmetrical facade, smooth wall surfaces with rounded corners, sparsity of ornamentation (often confined to horizontal grooves or metal strips on walls), flat roof, windows that frequently wrap around corners, and a curved canopy over the front door.

ash dump

The opening in the hearth into which ashes from the fireplace may be emptied to the ash pit below. The ash dump is usually fitted with a pivoting cover. See illustration on page 20.

ashlar

Squared building stone characterized by a high quality of finish and thin mortar joints. Also, in carpentry, a short stud between sloping rafters and joists; usually found near the eaves.

Synonyms: **ashler**

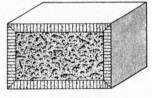

ashlar

ashlar masonry

Masonry composed of ashlar. Sometimes the term is used to include masonry composed of fired clay and shale, as well as stone. Ashlar masonry may be laid in one of three possible configurations:

- **broken range work**, where ashlar blocks of varying heights are laid in horizontal and intermittently broken courses

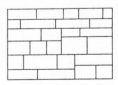

broken range work

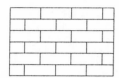

coursed range work

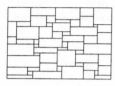

random range work

- **coursed** or **coursed range work**, where ashlar blocks are all of the same height and therefore form continuous horizontal joints

- **random range work, random work, broken ashlar, random range ashlar**, where blocks of varying heights and widths are laid in irregular (random) courses.

ash pit

A receptacle below the fireplace for receiving and storing ashes. A **clean out door** provides access to the pit for the removal of accumulated burned debris.

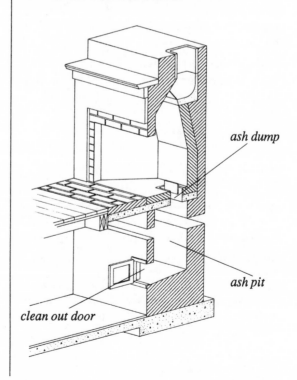

ash dump

ash pit

clean out door

astragal
A small molding that is semicircular in section; generally has a fillet on one or both sides; may be plain or ornamented.
Synonyms: **bead, baguette, bagnette**

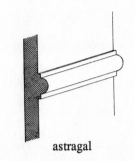

astragal

attic
In classical architecture, the space above the entablature or wall cornice; in modern usage, the room or space in the roof of a building; a **garret**. The term **knock-heads** is found in earlier literature for describing attics with sloping ceilings.

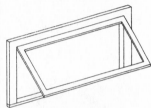

awning window

awning window
A window that is hinged at the top and swings outward.

backfill
Soil, sand, or other material used to fill an area that has been previously excavated, or such material used to slope or fill the ground around a structure so that water will drain away from the foundation; called **infill** in Great Britain.

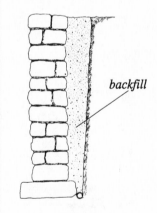

backfill

backing
Stone, brick, etc., forming the unexposed or unfinished wall behind the face stones; generally, backing is of an inferior or cheaper class of material. Backing also is used to describe the backfill of a retaining wall.

backing

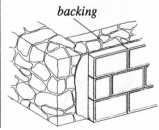

balconet

balconet
A low, slightly projecting, ornamental railing around the lower portion of a window; a false-balcony.

balcony
A railed projecting platform found above ground level on a building.

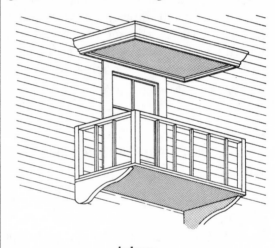

balcony

ballflower

ballflower
A small spherical ornament that is formed by three folds enclosing a ball; most often found in hollow molding.
Synonyms: **ball and flower**

balloon framing
A system of framing a building in which the studs extend in one piece from the top of the foundation sill plate to the top plate; floor joists are nailed to the studs and are supported by ledger boards (horizontal boards). Balloon framing was introduced in the early 1830s

and quickly replaced timber framing as the preferred framing method due to its ease of construction and lower material and construction costs.

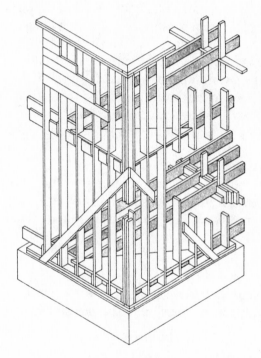

balloon framing

baluster

One of a series of short pillars or other uprights that support a handrail or coping. Balusters are often lathe-turned and vase-shaped in appearance, although they are also quite often simple square posts or cut outs.

baluster

balustrade

A series of balusters connected on top by coping or a handrail (top rail) and sometimes on the bottom by a bottom rail; used on staircases, balconies, porches, etc.

band

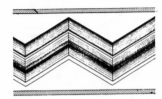

band
Any flat horizontal member that projects slightly from the surface of which it is a part; often used to mark a division in a wall. Sometimes the portion between bands is decorated with a variety of ornamental design elements, as seen in the illustration. Band is often used synonymously with the term **fillet**.
Synonyms: **band molding, band course**

banded column
A column in which the drums (sections) of the shaft alternate in size and often in texture.
Synonyms: **ringed column, rusticated column**

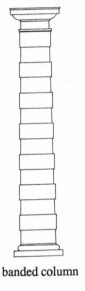

banded column

banister
A corruption of the word baluster; the term now generally refers to the balustrade of a staircase.

bargeboard
A sometimes richly ornamented board placed on the verge (incline) of the gable to conceal the ends of rafters.
Synonyms: **vergeboard, gableboard**

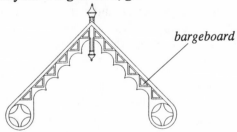

bargeboard

base
The lowest part of a column or architectural structure. See illustration on page 15.

baseboard
A plain or molded board that covers the gap between an interior wall or partition and the floor; also serves as a means of protecting the base of a wall from mopping, scuffing, kicking, etc.
Synonyms: **skirting, skirting board, mopboard, scrubboard, washboard, fascia**

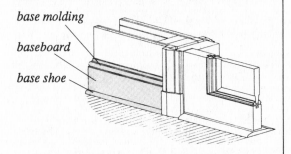

base molding

baseboard

base shoe

basement
The story below the main floor; may be partially or wholly below ground level.

base molding
A molded strip that runs along the top edge of a baseboard. See illustration above.
Synonyms: **base cap**

base shoe
A molded strip that conceals the gap between the bottom of the baseboard and the floor. See illustration above.

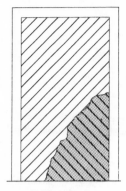

solid batten door

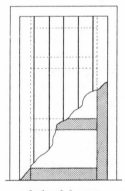

ledged door

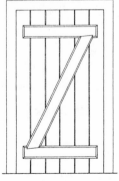

ledged and braced

Synonyms: **base shoe molding, shoe molding, floor molding, carpet strip, baseboard shoe**

bathroom
A room containing a water closet (toilet), a sink (lavatory),and a bathtub and/or shower. A **half-bath** contains only a water closet and a sink.

batten
A narrow board used to cover gaps between siding boards or sheathing; also used to brace and stiffen boards joined edge-to-edge, as in a batten door.

batten door
A door constructed by nailing boards (battens) together in various ways. The **solid batten door** or **double diagonal door** is composed of two layers of boards nailed at 90° to each other. The **ledged door, frontier door**, or **batten door** is made by securing vertical or diagonal battens to each other by horizontal members (ledge boards). This type of door may or may not be framed along its perimeter. The **ledged and braced door, braced door**, or **Z-pattern door** consists of horizontal members (ledges) that are secured to each other by diagonal members (braces).

battered wall
A wall that is thicker at the bottom than at the top. Battered walls are a common feature in Pueblo Revival architecture.

battled
Descriptive of anything having battlements.
See: crenelation.
Synonyms: **embattled**

bay
A space protruding from the exterior wall that
contains a bay window. Also, a compartment
of about 16 feet on a side.

bay leaf band
A banded garland of stylized laurel leaves
used as decoration for torus moldings.
Synonyms: **bay leaf garland**

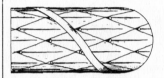
bay leaf band

bay window
A projecting window with an angular plan.

bead
A small convex molding that is semicircular
or greater in section. Beads are given specific
names according to their decorative treatment, use, and size. Bead moldings discussed
in this dictionary include: astragal, bead and
reel, pearl molding, quirk bead, flush bead,
reeding, and return bead.
Synonyms: **bead molding, astragal,
baguette, bagnette, half round**

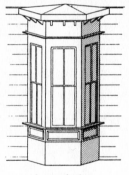
bay window

bead and reel
A molding consisting of alternating disks and
elongated beads.

bead and reel

beam
One of the principal horizontal timbers in a
wood framed building; its primary function

is to carry transverse loads such as floor joists or rafters.

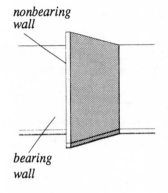

nonbearing wall

bearing wall

bearing wall
A wall that supports any vertical load (such as the floor, roof, or ceiling above) in addition to its own weight. A wall that does not support a vertical load is called a **nonbearing wall, nonbearing partition**, or simply **partition**.
Synonyms: **load-bearing wall**

Beaux Arts (1885 - 1925)
An architectural style characterized by: monumental and imposing appearance; symmetrical facade; wall surfaces embellished with floral patterns, garlands, medallions, or the like; exterior walls having quoins, pilasters, and paired colossal columns; flat, low-pitched, or mansard roofs; and a variety of stone finishes.

bedroom
A sleeping room in a building.

belcast gambrel roof

belcast eaves
A curve in the slope of a roof at the eaves; used not only because of its aesthetic appeal, but also because it protects the exterior walls from rainwater running off the roof. A **gambrel roof with belcast eaves** (sometimes called **belcast gambrel roof**) is illustrated, as well as a **hip roof with belcast eaves** (or a **belcast hip roof**).

belcast hip roof

birdsmouth
A V-shaped cut at the end of a structural member; typically found where a rafter meets the top sill of a wall.

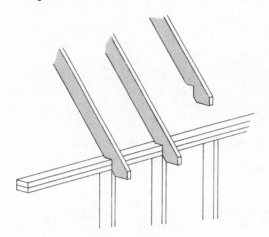

rafters with birdsmouth cuts

blocked
A joint formed by holding two abutting members together through the use of a third member.
Synonyms: **blocked joint**

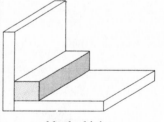

blocked joint

bolection molding
A molding used to conceal and decorate a joint caused by two surfaces coming together at different levels; found most frequently on panelwork.

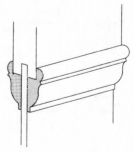

borning room
A room reserved for births. In the past the borning room was usually located near the kitchen so that hot water was readily available.

bolection molding

boss
A usually richly decorated projecting ornament placed at the intersection of beams or
ribs, or at the termination of a molding.

Boston hip
A method of finishing the joint (or hip) of a
shingled, slated, or tiled roof through the use
of two rows of overlapping shingles or flat
tiles.
Synonyms: **Boston hip roof, Boston ridge,
ridge row lap, shingle ridge finish**

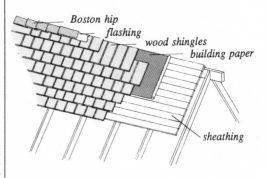

typical configuration for a Boston hip roof

bower
A garden shelter made of twisted vines or tree
branches; an attractive retreat or dwelling
place; an **arbor**.

bow window
A rounded bay window; a window forming
the segment of a circle.

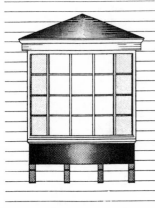

bow window

box stair
A stairway enclosed by walls or partitions. Generally, a box stair has a door opening at each floor level.
Synonyms: **boxed-in stair, closed stair**

brace
A piece of slanting timber used to stiffen or support some part of a structure. A short brace placed between, or across, the angle formed by two joining members is called a **knee brace**. A knee brace that supports a rafter is called a **strut**. Bracing that is sunk into vertical support members is sometimes called **let-in bracing**. See example on page 23.

braced framing
A framing system involving the use of corner posts and bracing.
Synonyms: **full framing**

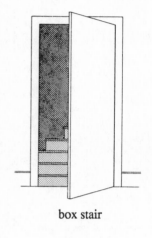

box stair

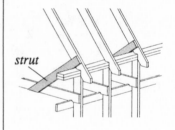

strut

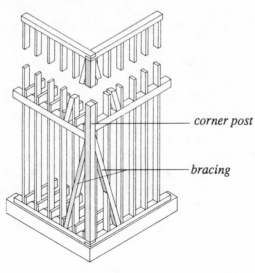

corner post

bracing

braced framing

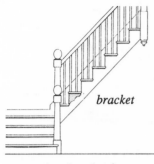

bracket

bracketed stair

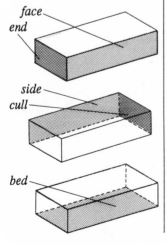

brackets

face
end

side
cull

bed

bracketed stair
A flight of open string stairs that are decorated with brackets on the exposed outer string.
Synonyms: **step brackets**

brackets
Projecting support members found under eaves or other overhangs; may be plain or decorated. Related terms: console, mutules, modillions, corbel.

brick
A usually rectangular building or paving unit made of fired clay; each unit is capable of being placed into position by the hands of one man. Bricks may be classified according to: place of manufacture, method of manufacture, chemical composition, size, shape, color, and intended use. Because distinctions between these classifications often become confusing (e.g., firebrick can be classified according to method of manufacture, size, shape, color, use, and place of manufacture) brick types are simply lumped into one classification under the heading **brick (types)**.

brick (surfaces)
Shown are the surfaces of a brick: the **face** (exposed long surface), the **end** (exposed short surface), the **side**, the **cull**, and the **bed** (top or bottom of a brick).

brick (types)
Bricks vary in appearance due to, among other factors, means of manufacture and in-

tended use. Below is a partial list of some common brick types:

- **bats.** Broken sections of bricks used to fill spaces or to form certain bonding patterns.

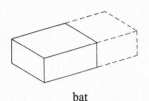
bat

- **bullnose, bullnose bricks.** Bricks with a rounded arris (edge); often found where a sharp edge would be undesirable.

- **carved bricks.** Bricks that are carved with a hammer or other tool and finished with a rubbing brick. **Carved brickwork** differs from **molded brickwork** in that solid brickwork is carved in place in the former; whereas bricks molded into specific shapes are built up to form a decorative design in the latter. See: **rubbed bricks.**

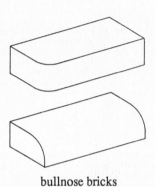
bullnose bricks

- **closers.** Cut or molded bricks in the form of half-headers. A half-header width, which is needed to complete various bonding patterns, can be accomplished through the use of either a **queen closer** (a half bat or two quarter bats) or a **king closer** (a three-quarter bat that exhibits a clipped header).

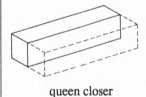
queen closer

- **common bricks.** Ordinary bricks intended for structural, not ornamental, purposes; used as backing for terra cotta, stone, and face brick, and for interior or exterior walls where appearance is not of great concern. As a

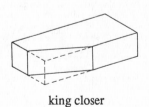
king closer

general rule, common bricks receive no special attention: they are not repressed, molded, rubbed, or carved. Common bricks often have surface imperfections such as kiss marks, grooves, and gouges.

• **dry-pressed bricks, pressed bricks.** Clay bricks made with only a small amount of water. They are compressed under high pressure which results in a very uniform brick with sharp edges and a surface sheen. Their fragile edges are susceptible to erosion due to a high clay to water ratio. Dry-pressed bricks are often used as face bricks.

• **face bricks, facing bricks, stone bricks.** Bricks used on the surfaces of walls. They differ from common bricks in that they exhibit a more even and uniform shape. Face bricks are often repressed.

• **firebricks.** Bricks made of a refractory clay that has great resistance to heat. They are used as a lining in fireplaces, chimneys, furnaces, and boilers. Firebrick clay contains very few or no impurities (which would lower their heat resisting qualities).

• **gauged bricks.** Sawn and rubbed, or ground, bricks made to precise (or *gauged*) dimensions. They are most often found in doorway or window ar-

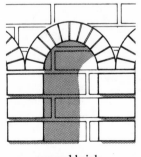

gauged brick

ches, in which case they are frequently referred to as **arch bricks.**

- **glazed bricks/enameled bricks.** Bricks with a glazed or enameled coating on one or more sides. Enameled bricks have a clear or colored glaze applied directly to the brick; whereas glazed bricks have a clear glaze applied over a white or colored intermediate slip (coating). Glazed bricks are found in bathrooms or other areas where easy cleaning or light reflecting qualities is important. Sometimes called **sanitary bricks.**

- **hand-made bricks.** Bricks molded by hand through the use of a wooden box, tray, etc., and then fired. Hand molding was the most popular way of making bricks up until the mid to late-1800s.

- **headers.** Bricks laid with their ends toward the face of a wall.

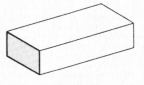

header

- **molded bricks.** Bricks that are molded into various decorative shapes before firing. They are used for cornices, moldings, and other built-up ornamental details.

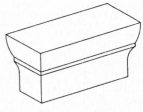

molded brick

- **repressed bricks.** After the initial molding, and while still in a plastic state, both hand and machine-made bricks may be *repressed* through the use of a repress machine. Besides producing slightly denser, more

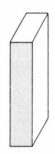

rowlock

soldier brick

squint brick

stretcher

uniform bricks, repressing is a means of impressing the company's name into the upper bed of the bricks. Because the pressure exerted by the repress machine is slight, the characteristic marks of the original manufacture are usually retained.

• **rowlock, rollock, rolock, rolok.** A term for describing bricks laid on edge rather than on bed.

• **rubbed bricks.** Bricks that are rubbed with an abrasive material to remove surface irregularities.

• **rustic bricks.** Face bricks with one or more surfaces either coated with sand or deliberately scratched before firing. Oftentimes such bricks are spotted or marked with various colors just before firing.

• **soldier bricks, soldiers.** A term for describing bricks laid on end so that their faces are positioned vertically on the wall surface.

• **squint bricks, squints.** Angularly-shaped bricks or other masonry units; commonly used in the construction of oblique wall corners.

• **stretchers.** Bricks laid with their sides toward the face of a wall.

- **wire-cut bricks.** Bricks made by extruding (or pressing) clay through an aperture and cutting the plastic mass into brick shapes by wires. Wire-cut bricks are less dense than dry-pressed bricks and often have striated surfaces caused by the extrusion process.

brickwork
Masonry construction in brick.

brickwork (bonding)
The term **bonding** in brickwork refers to the repeating arrangement of bricks into various patterns. Each of the twelve bonding patterns discussed below exhibit unique structural and decorative characteristics.

- **American bond, common bond, American common bond, English garden-wall bond, Liverpool bond.** A popular brickwork bond composed of either three or five courses of stretchers to each course of headers.

American bond

- **basket weave.** A bond composed of groups of two or three bricks laid perpendicular to all surrounding groups; commonly used for walls, walks, and interior and exterior floors.

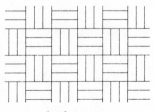

basket weave

- **dog-tooth, dog-tooth course.** A course of bricks laid diagonally on bed so that a corner of each brick projects beyond the wall surface; commonly used as a stringcourse.

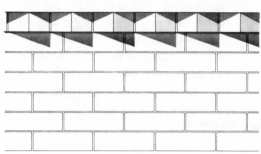

dog-tooth course

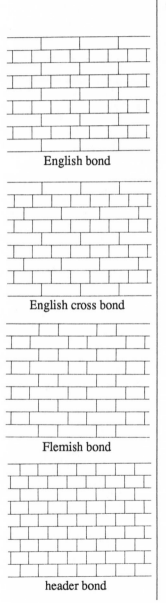

English bond

English cross bond

Flemish bond

header bond

- **English bond.** A strong but expensive bond composed of alternating courses of stretchers and headers. (Note that the bricks in all stretcher courses line up vertically.)

- **English cross bond.** A bond whose only difference from the English bond is that each alternate course of stretchers is moved over half the length of a brick.

- **Flemish bond.** In this bond, headers and stretchers alternate in each course with the center of each header over the center of the stretcher directly below it; more decorative but structurally weaker than English bond.

- **header bond, heading bond.** A bond consisting of nothing but headers in each course; used in sharply curving walls.

- **herringbone, herringbone work, herringbone brickwork.** A brickwork pattern characterized by courses laid diagonally and in opposite directions from adjacent courses; frequently used as a decorative device for floors and walls.

herringbone

- **honeycomb, honeycomb brickwork.** A brickwork bond characterized by the omission of certain bricks for decorative purposes, or to allow for better ventilation.

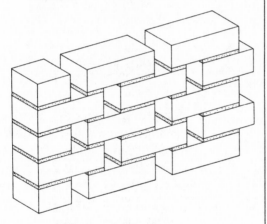

honeycomb brickwork

- **stack bond.** A bond composed of vertically aligned bricks; restricted to non load-bearing walls and partitions because of inherent weaknesses.

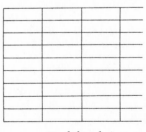

stack bond

- **rat-trap bond, Chinese bond, rowlock bond, silverlock bond.** A bond built up of rowlocks (bricks on edge) where each course consists of alternating headers and stretchers. Although a rat-trap wall uses fewer bricks to reach a given height, and is therefore cheaper to construct, it has the disadvantage of being weak and susceptible to moisture penetration.

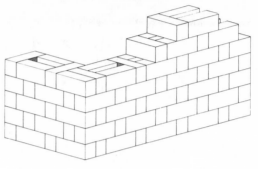

rat-trap bond

• **stretcher bond, stretching bond.** A bond consisting of only stretchers; each alternate course of stretchers is moved over half the length of a brick. **Raking stretcher bond,** or **1/3** (one-third) **running bond,** differs from a stretcher bond in that each alternate course of stretchers is moved over less than half the length of a brick. Stretcher bond and raking stretcher bond are rarely used for solid walls because they lack headers which serve as bonding bricks for such walls.

stretcher bond

raking stretcher bond

block bridging

bridging
A brace, or series of braces, placed between joists, studs, or other structural members. **Block bridging** (also called **solid bridging,**

solid strutting, or **blocking**) consists of short vertically positioned blocks of wood between floor joists, or the like. **Cross bridging** consists of metal straps or small pieces of wood that cross each other diagonally between joists. Bridging, in general, serves to stiffen structural members and distribute the load.

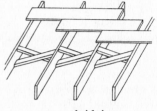

cross bridging

bridle joint

A joint composed of one double-tongued and one double-slotted member.

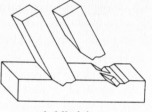

bridle joint

brownstone

A predominantly brown sandstone used early on in American architecture for general construction.

building paper

A usually tar-impregnated sheathing paper used on roofs and walls of buildings as a means of protection against dampness, dirt, cold, dust, and wind.
Synonyms: **felt paper, tar paper, black paper**

bulkhead door

A door that provides exterior access to a cellar.

bulkhead door

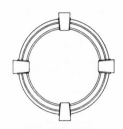

bull's eye, oculus

side light with rondels

bull's eye
A round or oval panel or aperture. In the latter case, it may be glazed, open, or louvered. A bull's eye is often encircled by a double arched frame with voussoirs. A **rondel** (or **roundel**) is a small bull's eye or circular panel; in glazing it looks something like the bottom of a bottle.
Synonyms: **oculus**

Bungalow (1890 - 1940)
An architectural style characterized by: small size, overall simplicity, broad gables (usually facing the street), dormer windows, porches with large square piers or elephantine (battered) porch posts, and exposed structural members or stickwork. This style varies greatly according to geographical location and date of construction. Houses characteristic of this style are often termed **bungaloid**.

buttery
A room for the storage and distribution of alcoholic beverages; a room for storing the servant's utensils and supplies; a **pantry**.

butt joint
A joint formed when two members simply abut one another.

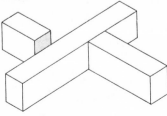

butt joint

cabinet
A private room for writing, studying, or conferring; a room for preserving or exhibiting curiosities or precious possessions. Also, a storage case.

cabling
An ornament resembling a cable or rope with twisted strands.

Synonyms: **cable molding, rope molding**

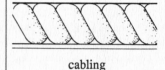

cabling

canale
A metal lined water spout that is carved into a vega (rounded roof beam); found in pueblo style architecture of the Southwest.

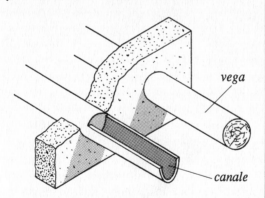

vega

canale

canale and vega

canopy
A projection over a niche or doorway; often decorative or decorated.

cant molding
A square molding in which the outer face is beveled.

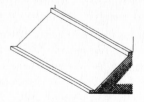

cant molding

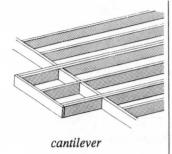

cantilever

cartouche

cantilever
A projecting beam, girder, or other structural member supported only at one end; used to support a balcony, cornice, extended eaves, or any other extension to a building or structure.

capital
The upper decorated portion of a column or pilaster on which the entablature rests. See illustration on page 15.
Synonyms: **chapiter**

carriage
The framing members that support the treads (steps) of a staircase.
Synonyms: **horse, springing tree, rough stringer, carrier**

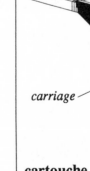

carriage

cartouche
An ornamental panel that is circular, oval, or scroll-like in shape.
Synonyms: **inscription stone, date stone**

casement
A window sash that opens on hinges fixed to its vertical edge.

casement window
A window containing two casements separated by a mullion (vertical dividing bar).

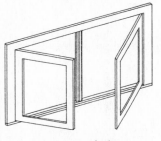

casement window

casing
The finished visible framework around a door or window.
Synonyms: **door casing, window casing**

cavetto
A concave molding that is about a quarter circle or quarter ellipse in section.

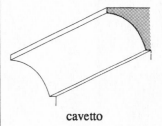

cavetto

cavity wall
An exterior wall consisting of two leaves linked by galvanized metal or iron wall ties; the cavity between the two leaves may or may not contain thermal insulating or moisture-proofing material. The rat-trap bonded wall, discussed under **brickwork (bonding)**, is an example of a **brick bonded** (versus **wall tie bonded**) **cavity wall**.
Synonyms: **hollow wall, hollow masonry wall**

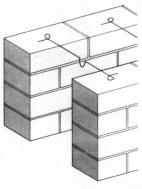

cavity wall (wall tie bonded)

ceiling
The overhead surface in a room. Some commonly encountered types of ceilings are: plain plaster, decorative plaster, wood strip, wood panel, and metal.

cellar
A room beneath the main floor of a building used for storage or provisions, wine, coal, etc.; sometimes used for cooking.

cement
Any material, or mixture of materials (such as clay and limestone), used in a plastic state and then allowed to harden in place. Cement is frequently combined with an aggregate (such as sand or gravel) to form concrete.

cement mortar
A mixture of cement, lime, sand, or other aggregates with water; used in plastering and bricklaying.

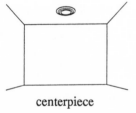

centerpiece

centerpiece
An ornament located in the center of a ceiling; often lavishly decorated.
Synonyms: **center, ceiling medallion, medallion, rosette**

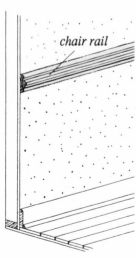

chair rail

chair rail
A wooden molding that runs along an interior wall at the level of the back of a chair; acts to protect plastered or papered walls from accidental scuffing or tearing by the backs of chairs. In houses with interior wall paneling the chair rail serves as the crowning member of the dado.
Synonyms: **dado rail**

chamber
A sleeping room or private living space. Also, any room above the cellar.

chamfer
A beveled edge on the corner of a post, wall, etc.; may take the form of a flat surface, a grooved surface, or a more elaborately molded surface. Edges so beveled are said to be **chamfered**.
Synonyms: **champher**

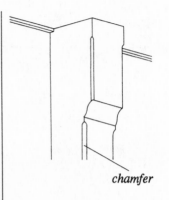

chamfer

channel
A groove cut or molded into an architectural member. A series of such grooves, such as found on some columns and pilasters, is called **channeling**.

Chateauesque (1860 - 1910)
An architectural style characterized by: massiveness, a steeply pitched hip or gable roof with many vertical elements (e.g., hip knobs with finials, tall decoratively treated chimneys, turrets, spires, etc.), roof cresting, multiple dormer windows (including wall dormers), towers, balconies, balconets, and masonry walls.

channels

chevron
A V-shaped decoration usually used in series; found most often on moldings.
Synonyms: **zigzag**

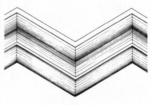

chevron or zigzag

chimney
A structure containing one or more flues through which smoke and fumes from fireplaces, furnaces, or boilers escape to the outside. A chimney also provides a draft for fireplaces.

chimney bar

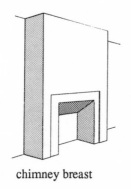
chimney breast

chimney cap

chimney bar
A horizontal metal bar above a fireplace opening that supports the masonry above. Before the early-1800s this horizontal member often consisted of an oak, or other hardwood, beam and was called a **manteltree**.
Synonyms: **chimney bar**

chimney breast
The portion of a fireplace and its walls that project into a room; this projection creates recesses (inglenooks) on one or both sides of the fireplace.

chimney cap
A concrete capping around the top of a chimney; acts to protect the top course of bricks from weather damage.

chimney hood
A concrete or stone slab, or other covering, that protects the chimney opening.

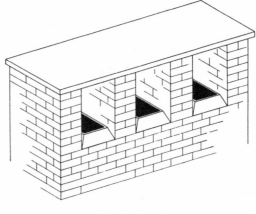
chimney hood

chimney pot
A terra cotta, brick, or metal pipe that is placed on the top of a chimney as a means of increasing the draft; often decoratively treated.
Synonyms: **chimney can**

chimney shaft
That part of the chimney visible above the roof surface.

cistern
A receptacle for the collection of rainwater or spring water; a storage tank for water or other liquids (e.g., the reservoir for a water closet).

clay tile flooring
Burnt clay tiles made in various sizes and thicknesses; usually laid on a concrete base; most frequently used for bathrooms, porches, vestibules, halls, and fireplace hearths.
Synonyms: **ceramic tile flooring**

closet
A small enclosed room or space used for storage (e.g., a coat closet, walk-in wardrobe, etc.).

coffering
Decoration on a ceiling formed by sometimes highly ornamented recessed panels.
Synonyms: **coffered ceiling, ceiling panels**

cogged joint
A joint formed when two members cross one another; both members are notched so that

chimney pot

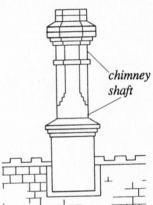

chimney shaft

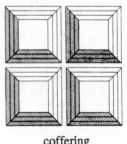

coffering

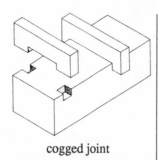

cogged joint

slippage or movement is prevented. This type of joinery is referred to as **cogging, cocking,** and sometimes **caulking.**

collar beam
A horizontal member that connects two opposite rafters at a level well above the top plate.
Synonyms: **top beam, spanpiece, sparpiece, wind beam**

collar beam roof
A roof in which rafters are tied together and stiffened by collar beams.
Synonyms: **collar roof**

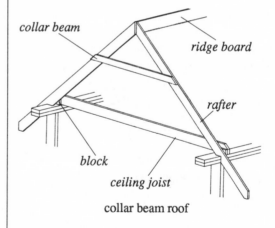

collar beam

ridge board

rafter

block

ceiling joist

collar beam roof

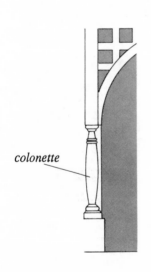

colonette

colonette
A small or slender column, usually decorative in nature.

colonial panel door
A door characterized by recessed panels that are framed by stiles (vertical members), rails

(horizontal members), and muntin (central member). When the stiles and rails of such a door form a cross, and the two bottom panels appear as an open book, the door is sometimes called a **cross and bible** or **Christian door**. See illustration on page 171.

Colonial Revival (1870 - 1950)
An architectural style characterized by: a balanced facade; the use of decorative door crowns and pediments, sidelights, fanlights, and porticos to emphasize the front entrance; double hung windows with multiple panes in one or both sashes; and frequent use of stringcourses or decorative cornices.

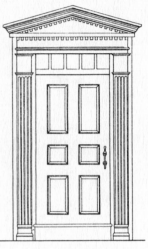

colonial panel door

colonnade
A series of regularly spaced columns; an open passageway with columns.

colossal column
A column that reaches more than one story in height.

column
A pillar, usually circular in plan. The parts of a column in classical architecture are the **base, shaft,** and **capital**. See illustration on page 15.

colossal column

compass roof
A roof characterized by having curved rafters or tie beams; A roof where the trusses form an arch.

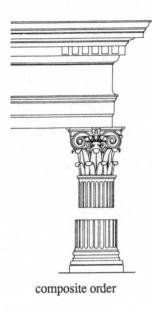

composite order

composite order
A classical order that incorporates the large volutes (spirals) of the Ionic capital with the lush foliage of the Corinthian capital.

compound arch
An arched entry formed by a series of concentric and progressively smaller arches set within one another.

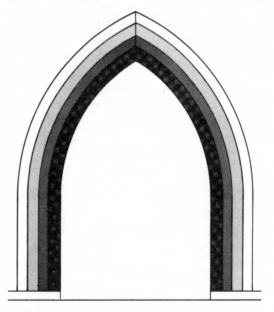

compound arch

concrete
A material that, when hardened, possesses great structural strength; made by mixing cement or mortar with water and frequently with various aggregates (such as sand, gravel, pebbles or shale). See: cement, cement mortar, mortar, portland cement.

concrete block
A hollow or solid rectangular block made of portland cement, aggregates, water, and often other admixtures; used in the construction of walls, foundations, piers, chimneys, etc. Beginning in the 1870s, concrete block was molded to imitate stone. Called **imitation stone block, imitation stone,** or **artistic concrete block,** this inexpensive substitute for stone facing took on a myriad of surface textures. Five popular styles are illustrated. They are (from top to bottom): *rock-faced, plain-faced with exposed aggregate, panel-faced, (vertical) tooled,* and *brush hammered face with tooled draft.* Due largely to quality control problems, imitation stone block fell out of favor as a cheap building material in the 1920s.
Synonyms: **cinder block**

concrete brick
A masonry unit constructed of concrete and in the form of a brick.

concrete flooring
A concrete floor placed directly on earth or on a tamped cinder or gravel base.
Synonyms: **slab flooring**

conical roof
A cone-shaped roof.

conservatory
A glass-enclosed room or greenhouse used to cultivate and display plants.

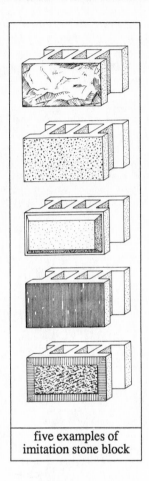

five examples of
imitation stone block

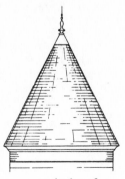

conical roof

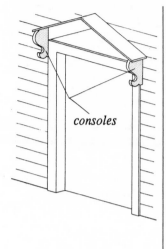

consoles

console

An ornamental bracket with an "S" or scroll-shaped form; used to support a door or window hood, a cornice, a piece of sculpture, etc.

coping

The protective uppermost course of a wall or parapet; projects beyond the wall surface to throw off rain. A commonly encountered sloping-topped coping is the **saddlebacked coping, saddle coping,** or simply **saddleback**.
Synonyms: **cap**

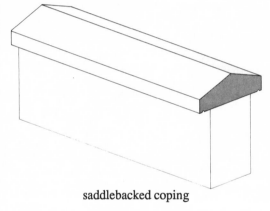

saddlebacked coping

corbel

A projecting block, sometimes carved or molded, that acts as a means of support for floor and roof beams as well as other structural members.

corbel arch

An arch-like construction composed of courses of masonry advancing inward as they rise on both sides of a wall opening.
Synonyms: **corbeled arch**

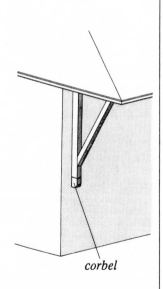

corbel

corbelling
A series of projections, each stepped out further than the one below it; most often found on walls and chimney stacks.

corbel table
A course projecting from a wall that is supported by a series of corbels. Corbel tables usually take on a simple stepped block form, but they may also be treated more decoratively, such as seen with the **arcaded corbel table**.

Corinthian order

corbel table

corbiestep
A gable with stepped sides; used to mask a pitched roof.
Synonyms: **catstep, crowstep, corbel-step**

Corinthian order
A classical order characterized by slender fluted columns and ornate capitals decorated with stylized acanthus leaves.

corbiestep

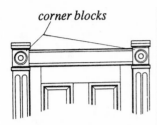

corner blocks

corner blocks
Blocks positioned at the corners of either window or door casings; often treated with design elements such as paterae (oval disks).

corner boards
Boards placed at the corners of exterior walls to provide a neater appearance and to protect the ends of the wood siding.

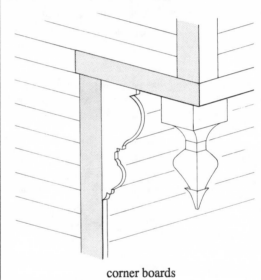

corner boards

cornice
The projection at the top of a wall; the top course or molding of a wall when it serves as a crowning member. Two general types of cornices are the **box cornice** and the **open cornice**. A cornice along the slope (rake) of a gable or pediment is termed a **raking cornice**. Also, the upper projection of the Entablature in classical architecture. See illustration on page 15.
Synonyms: **jet**

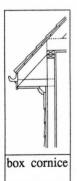

box cornice

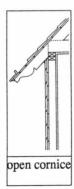

open cornice

corona
In classical architecture and its derivatives, the overhanging part of the cornice; framed by the cymatium and supported by bed molding beneath. See illustration on page 15.

coupled columns
Paired columns.

coupled windows
Two closely spaced windows that function independently but visually form a pair.

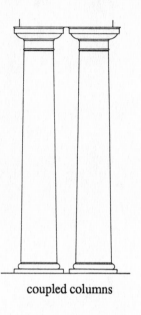

coupled columns

coupled windows

course
A horizontal row of bricks, stones, or other masonry units. The meaning of the term is often extended to include any material arranged in a row (e.g., roof shingles).

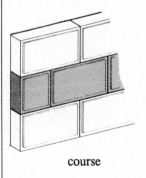

course

court
An open area partially or totally surrounded by walls or buildings.

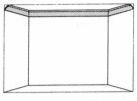

cove or cove molding

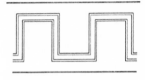

crenelation

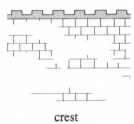

crest

cricket

cove
A concave or canted molding located in the area of transition between wall and ceiling. A **cove ceiling** is one in which there is a smooth concave transition between wall and ceiling. Synonyms: **cove molding**

crawl space
The shallow space beneath the first floor of a house with no basement; used for visual inspection of, and access to, ducts and pipes.

crenelation
Any decorative element that simulates the squares (merlons) and the spaces (embrasures, crenels) of a defensive parapet; moldings so decorated are said to be **crenelated moldings** or **embattled moldings. Exterior trim, such as bargeboards, may also be crenelated.**

crest
The ornamental work forming the top of a screen or wall, or the decorative railing running along the ridge of a roof; oftentimes perforated as well as decorated. A crest differs from a ridgecap in that the former is employed as a decorative device, the latter as a means of covering the ridge of a roof. Synonyms: **cresting**

cricket
A small structure behind a chimney stack that is designed to direct water away from the chimney.

cripple
A short structural member. **Cripple studs** are often found above or below wall openings; **cripple rafters** (or **jack rafters**) are found extending from hip rafters and valley rafters. See illustrations on pages 83 and 132.

crown
The top of an arch or vault. Also, any uppermost or terminal feature in architecture.

crown molding
The crowning or finishing molding; most often located in the area of transition between wall and ceiling, or on the extreme top edge of an exterior wall.

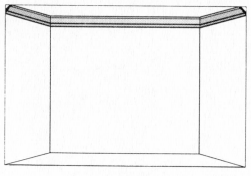

crown molding

cupboard
A small closet or cabinet, usually with shelves, used for the storage of kitchenware, etc.

curb roof
A pitched roof characterized by two sloping surfaces.

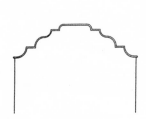

curvilinear gable

curtain wall
A thin, exterior, nonbearing wall between columns and piers in a skeleton frame. Such a wall is wholly supported at each story and is therefore not dependent on the load-bearing quality of the wall directly below it.

curvilinear gable
A gable that has multiple curving sides.
Synonyms: **Dutch gable, Dutch roof**

cutaway corner
A corner formed by the meeting of three wall surfaces; often embellished with corner brackets.

cutaway corner

cut roof
A pitched roof with a truncated (flattened) top instead of a ridge.
Synonyms: **truncated roof, terrace roof**

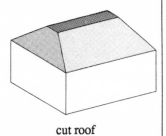

cut roof

cyma recta
A double-curved molding that is concave on the upper portion and convex on the lower portion.
Synonyms: **sima recta, ogee molding**

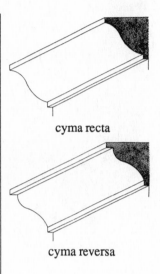
cyma recta

cyma reversa
A double-curved molding that is convex on the upper portion and concave on the lower portion.
Synonyms: **sima reversa, reverse ogee molding**

cyma reversa

cymatium
In classical architecture and its derivatives, the crowning molding on a cornice; usually in the form of a cyma reversa, but can also be found in the form of an ovolo or cavetto. See illustration on page 15.

dado
The middle portion of a pedestal between the base and surbase. See illustration on page 15. In modern usage, dado refers to the part of the finishing found on the lower portion of an interior wall or partition; may be plain, or decorated with paneling or the like. When wood paneling or other facing material is used which differs from the material used on the rest of the wall, the dado is often referred to as **wainscot** or **wainscotting**.

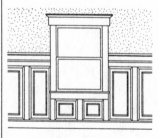
dado or wainscot

dado and rabbet
A joint composed of a combination of a dado (housed) joint and a rabbet joint.

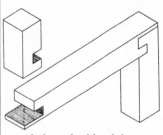
dado and rabbet joint

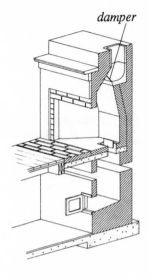

damper

damper
A pivoting metal plate above the fireplace that is designed to regulate draft.

decorative half-timbering
A method of surface decoration that imitates true half-timber construction. See: half-timbering. Decorative half-timbering differs from stickwork in that the former involves the placement of non-structural horizontal, vertical, and curvilinear wood elements on a brick or stucco wall; whereas the latter incorporates horizontal and vertical wood members for structural as well as decorative reasons.

decorative half-timbering

den
A usually small room used for work, study, or leisure.

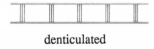

denticulated

denticulated
That which is embellished with dentils or dentil-like ornamentation.
Synonyms: **denticular**

dentils
Small square blocks found in series on many cornices, moldings, etc.

dependency
An ancillary structure adjoining, or in close proximity to, a main building.

diamond notch
A corner notch characterized by a diamond-shaped tongue.

diaper
A decorative field usually consisting of squares, lozenges, or diamonds; often found on wall surfaces.
Synonyms: **diaper work**

dogleg stair
A stair with no wellhole between flights.

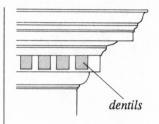

dentils

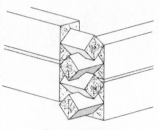

diamond notch

diaper

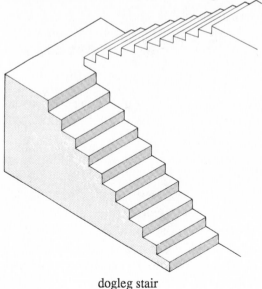

dogleg stair

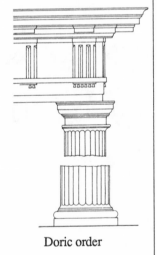

Doric order

door
A movable barrier that allows or limits access into a building or into any space within a building. For the parts of a door see: door stop, muntin, rail, stile, threshold, panel, doorframe. For types of doors see: batten door, bulkhead door, colonial panel door, Dutch door, flush door, half-glass door, paneled door, screen door, sliding door, trapdoor.

doorframe
That part of a door opening to which a door is hinged. A doorframe consists of two vertical members called **jambs** (also called **doorjambs, doorcheeks, doorposts,** or **door trees**), and a horizontal top member called a **lintel** (also called **door head, head jamb,** or **header**). See illustration on page 83.

door stop
The vertical strip against which a door slams. Synonyms: **door bumper, slamming stile**

Doric order
A classical order characterized by overall simplicity, a plain capital, heavy fluted columns, and no base.

dormer
A vertical window projecting from the slope of a roof; usually provided with its own roof. The specific name of a dormer is frequently determined by the shape or type of its roof: the **eyelid** or **eyebrow dormer** has an arched roof that gives it the appearance of an eyelid;

the **shed dormer** and the **gable dormer** are so named because of their shed and gable roofs. A **wall dormer** is a dormer that is flush with the face of a building.
Synonyms: **dormer window, Lutheran window**

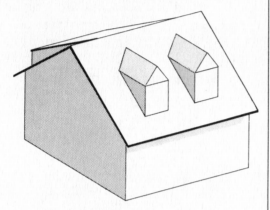

shed dormer and two gable dormers

double hung window

double hung window
A window with two sashes, each movable by means of sash cords and weights.

double notch
A corner notch formed by cutting square depressions on the tops and bottoms of timbers or logs; cuts are located near the ends of the members.

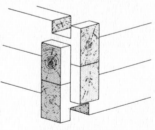

double notch

dovetail joint
A joint formed by two interlocking elements: a wedge-shaped tenon and a corresponding mortise; used extensively for joining corners in cabinet making; also used for securing structural members in timber frame construc-

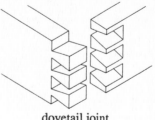

dovetail joint

tion. When both edges of the tenon are cut at an angle, as mentioned above, the joint is termed a **full-dovetail**, or simply **dovetail**; when only one edge is cut, the joint is termed a **half-dovetail**; when more than just the tenon is carried by the mortised member, the joint is called a **shouldered dovetail**; and when one-half of the thickness of the tenon is cut away, the joint is termed a **dovetail half-lap joint**.
Synonyms: **dovetailed joint, dovetail**

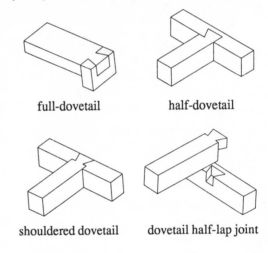

full-dovetail   half-dovetail

shouldered dovetail   dovetail half-lap joint

dovetail notch
A corner notch in the form of a dovetail. Full-dovetail and half-dovetail notches are illustrated.

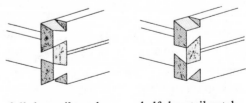

full-dovetail notch   half-dovetail notch

doweling

A method of securing two members together through the use of dowels (pins).

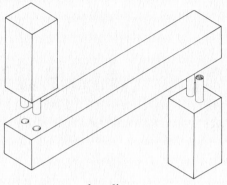

doweling

downspout

A pipe that carries water from the gutters to the ground, or to a sewer connection.

Synonyms: **leader, downspout leader, conductor**

draintile

Burnt clay or concrete pipe placed on a gravel bed at the level of the footing; used to drain subsurface water away from foundations and basement walls.

drip

A projecting molding found over doors, windows, and archways; used to direct rain away from the wall opening. A rectangular drip is frequently called a **label molding.**

Synonyms: **hood mold, head mold, drip hood mold, hood molding, weather molding**

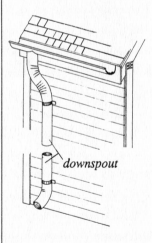

downspout

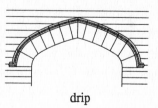

drip

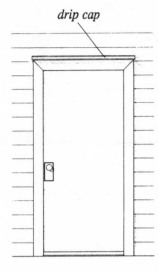

drip cap

drip cap
A usually small horizontal drip located above a door or window casing; designed to shed water, causing it to drip beyond the outside of the frame.

drop
A small, often tear-shaped, ornament found on the bottom of a newel, below a wall overhang, on a bargeboard, etc.; a pendant.
Synonyms: **drop ornament, droop**

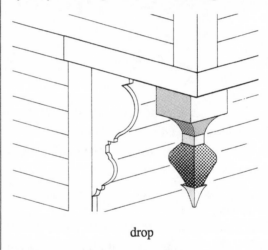

drop

Dutch Colonial (1625 - 1830)
An architectural style characterized by: a steeply pitched gable or gambrel roof with a pronounced eave overhang, Dutch (double) doors, and commonly six-over-six double hung windows with exterior shutters.

Dutch door
A door consisting of two leaves (sections); the leaves may be opened together or separately.

Dutch door

easement
A curve in a handrail; found where the descending rail meets the newel.
Synonyms: **ease**

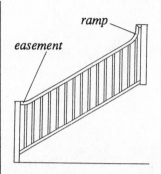
easement

Eastern Stick (1860 - ca. 1900)
An architectural style characterized by: asymmetry and angularity, stickwork (i.e., narrow boards nailed to the exterior walls so as to repeat and reinforce the structural skeleton), verandas with diagonal braces, steeply pitched intersecting gable roofs, wood siding (usually board and batten or clapboard), and gable trim.

eave
That portion of the roof which projects beyond the walls. Eaves that are without gutters are often referred to as **dripping eaves**.
Synonyms: **eaves**

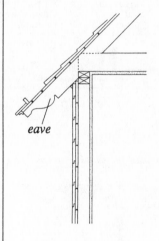
eave

echinus
The convex molding located just below the abacus on the capital of a column. See illustration on page 15.

eclecticism
As it pertains to architecture: the free use and mixture of forms and details from any historic style; especially prevalent in the latter part of the nineteenth century in the United States.

egg and dart
An ovolo molding made up of alternating egg-shaped and dart-shaped elements.
Synonyms: **egg and tongue**

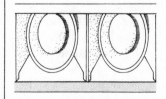
egg and dart

elephantine columns
Broad, square columns that taper toward the top; such columns are the trademark of bungalow style homes of the early-twentieth century.
Synonyms: **tapered posts, tapered columns, tapered pillars**

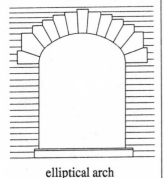

elliptical arch

ell
An extension that is at right angles to the length of a building.

elliptical arch
An arch formed either by true elliptic curves or by usually three circular arcs. In the latter case it is sometimes called a **three centered arch**.

embellishment
Adornment with decorative elements; ornamentation.
Synonyms: **enrichment**

embrasure
An enlarged door or window opening with slanted sides on the inside face making its interior dimensions greater than those of its exterior.

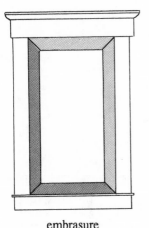

embrasure

encaustic
Glazed and decorated earthenware tile used for floors.
Synonyms: **encaustic tile**

engaged column
A column that is in direct contact with a wall; at least half of the column projects beyond the surface of the wall to which it is engaged.

entablature
In classical architecture and derivatives, the part of a building carried by the columns; consists of **cornice, frieze,** and **architrave.**

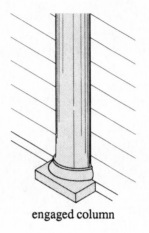

engaged column

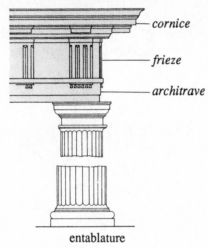

entablature

entasis
In classical architecture, the slight convex curve of the shaft of a column. The Greeks were the first to use convexly-curved columns as a means of correcting the optical illusion of concavity which resulted from the placement of straight-sided columns in close proximity to one another.

entry
The entrance to a building, such as a gate, foyer, or hall.

Exotic Revivals (1835 - 1930)
Architectural styles borrowing elements from "exotic" cultures. The **Egyptian Revival** is probably the best known from this group. It is easily identified by massive columns that resemble a bundle of stalks tied together and bulging at the top. Moorish and Turkish architectural traditions also influenced design in America.

extrados
The outermost curve of an arch or vault.

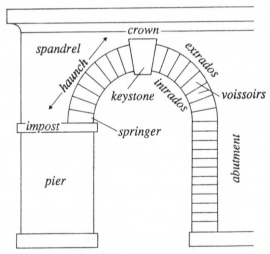

the parts of an arched opening

facade, façade
The principal face or front elevation of a building.

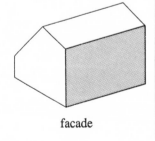

facade

face stones, face bricks
The exposed stones or bricks of a wall.

facing

Any non-structural material (e.g., wood, stucco, plaster, metal, terra cotta, etc.) that acts to cover a less attractive or rougher wall surface.
Synonyms: **facework**

fanlight

A semicircular or fan-shaped window with a radiating glazing bar system; usually found over entrance doors.

fanlight

fascia

The flat member of the architrave in classical architecture. See illustration on page 15.

fascia board

A flat board used to cover the ends of roof rafters.
Synonyms: **eaves fascia, fascia**

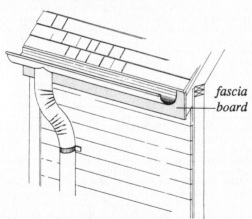
fascia board

Federal, Adam (1780 - 1830)

An architectural style characterized by: overall symmetry, semi-circular or elliptical fanlight over a six-panel front door, elaborate door trim (including columns or pilasters), decorated (often denticulated) cornice, six-paned double hung windows arranged most often in five bays, and slender end chimneys.

fenestration
The arrangement of windows and other exterior openings on a building.

festoon
A molded, carved, or painted ornament in the form of a garland of fruit and flowers, or sometimes ripe oats, which is tied or suspended at its two ends; often found on a frieze.

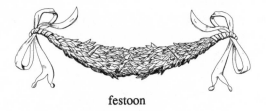

festoon

field stone

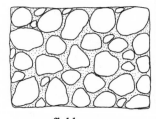

field stone

Small uncut boulders or large stones used in their natural form for fences, crude walls, and so on. Such stonework usually involves the use of large amounts of mortar to fill in the gaps left between adjoining stones. Sometimes a distinction is made between **plain** (uncut) **field stone** and **split field stone** (i.e., where the exposed face of the stone is cut or dressed).

figure
the natural pattern in wood caused by such

factors as color differences between heartwood and sapwood, or growth rings; quite often exploited ornamentally.

fillet

A small, flat band used between the flutes of a column, or between moldings, as a separator. Sometimes a distinction is made between a **raised** (projecting) **fillet** and a **sunk** (recessed) **fillet**.

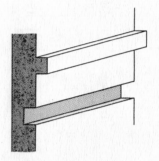

raised and sunk fillets

finger joint

A heading joint consisting of two serrated members joined end-to-end.
Synonyms: **serrate**

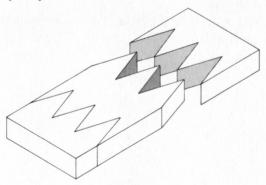

finger joint

finial

An ornament that caps a gable, hip, pinnacle, or other architectural feature. The term **urn** is used if the finial is vase-shaped. When a finial is used on a gable with a bargeboard, it is generally terminated with a pendant. Sometimes the term **hip knob** is used to refer to a simple finial placed on the hip of a roof.

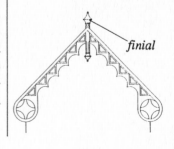

finial

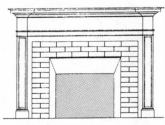

fireback

fireback
The back wall of the fireplace, especially when constructed of ornamental cast or wrought metal; serves to improve the appearance and radiate heat into the room. Synonyms: **chimney back**

fireboard
A board, screen, or other device used to close off a fireplace opening when not in use.

fire frame
An iron housing set into a fireplace to reduce its size.

fireplace
The opening at the base of a chimney where the fire is built. The parts of a fireplace are shown below.

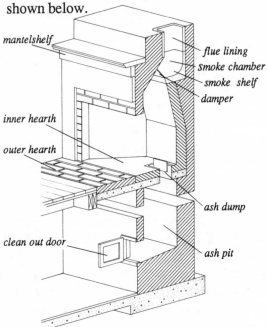

fishplate
A method of securing two members together, end-to-end, through the use of wood or metal plates; may be either nailed or bolted.
Synonyms: **fished joint**

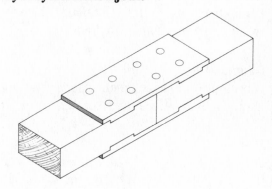

fishplate

fixed sash
A fixed frame window (or a part of a window) that does not open.

Synonyms: **fixed light, deadlight**

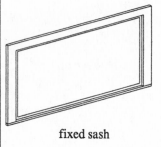

fixed sash

flashing
Pieces of noncorrosive metal used around wall and roof junctions and angles as a means of preventing leaks. See drawing, page 30.

flagstone
A naturally occurring, split or sawn, flat stone; used frequently for walks and patio or terrace paving.

flat arch
An arch with a flat intrados (underside). The term **soldier arch** is usually reserved for a flat

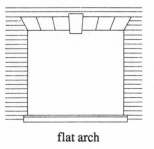

flat arch

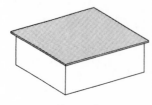

flat roof

fleur-de-lis

arch built of soldiers (bricks laid vertically).
Synonyms: **jack arch, straight arch, French arch, soldier arch**

flat roof
A roof that has only enough pitch so that rain water or melting snow can drain.

fleur-de-lis
A decorative design element resembling long leaves bound together by a band.

flier
Any of the steps in a flight of stairs whose treads are parallel and of uniform width. See illustration below.
Synonyms: **flier**

flight of stairs
A single set of stairs running from floor to floor, or from floor to landing.
Synonyms: **stairway**

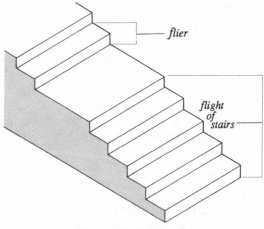

flier and flight of stairs

flooring

A floor, or the materials used for a floor. In this book, four major categories of flooring are discussed: clay tile flooring, concrete flooring, resilient flooring, and wood flooring.

flue

An enclosed passageway in a chimney for the conveyance of smoke and gasses to the outside.
Synonyms: **chimney flue**

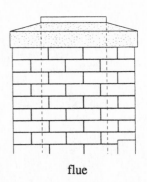

flue

flue lining

Rectangular or round tile (or other heat-resistant materials) used in the chimney flue for protective purposes. See drawing, page 76.
Synonyms: **chimney lining**

flush bead

A small convex molding set into the surrounding surface so as to be flush with that surface.
Synonyms: **recessed bead, sunk bead, double quirked bead**

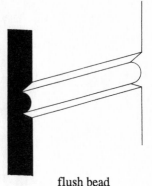

flush bead

flush door

A door with plain flat surfaces.

fluting

Vertical, concave channels on columns, pilasters, and other surfaces. See illustration of channeling on page 47.

foliation

Ornamentation resembling leaves.

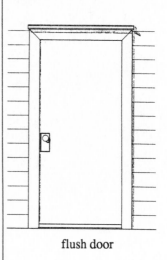

flush door

Folk Victorian (1870 - 1915)
An architectural style characterized by over-all simplicity of form. Decorative treatment is usually confined to porch trim, gable trim, and brackets under the eaves.

footing
An enlargement at the base of a foundation wall or pier; its function is to transmit the superimposed load to the soil below. A footing is generally made of concrete, but may also be made of timber, iron, or large flat stones. Note that the **pile foundation** — a **pile** is a long wood or metal beam driven into the ground — is friction-supported and therefore requires no footing.

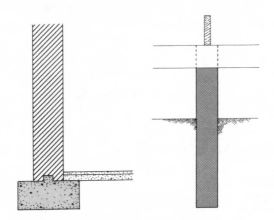

footing (left) pile (right)

foundation
The part of a structure that is in direct contact with the ground and serves to transmit the load of the structure to the earth; the substructure of a building (consisting of the foundation walls and footings). A foundation which consists of a poured concrete slab is called a

slab foundation, slab-on-ground foundation, or slab-on-grade foundation.

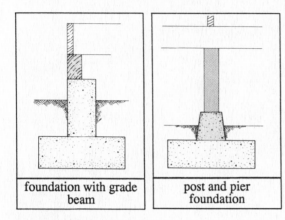

| foundation with grade beam | post and pier foundation |

foundation walls
Poured concrete, concrete block, brick, or rubble masonry walls that enclose a basement or crawl space and support the parts of a building that are above grade. Illustrated (left to right) is a **brick masonry foundation wall**, a **rubble masonry foundation wall**, and a **poured concrete foundation wall**.

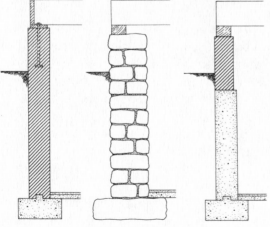

three typical foundation systems

four centered arch
A shallow, pointed arch formed by four circular arcs.
Synonyms: **depressed arch**

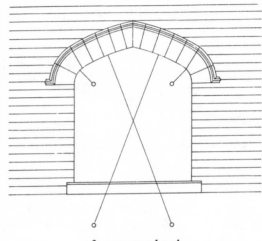

four centered arch

foyer
An entrance space between the outside and interior rooms of a building.

frame construction
A building consisting primarily or entirely of wood structural members. The illustration on the following page shows the more commonly encountered structural members found in frame construction.
Synonyms: **wood frame construction, frame structure**

framework
The various supporting members that, when joined together, form the skeleton of a building.

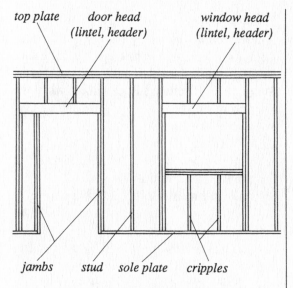

top plate   door head   window head
             (lintel, header) (lintel, header)

jambs   stud   sole plate   cripples

some common structural members in frame
construction

framing system

A method of constructing the skeletal
framework of a building. Four systems for
constructing a wood frame structure are discussed in this book: balloon framing, braced
framing, platform framing, and timber framing.

French Colonial (1700 - 1830)

An architectural style characterized by: narrow door and window openings, paired casement windows with exterior shutters, paired
French doors, steeply pitched hipped or belcast gable roof, and half-timber framing with
a stucco covering. In rural areas the main
floor is often raised and has and extended
porch (called a galerie).

French door

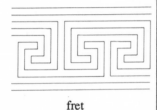

fret

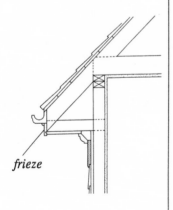

frieze

French door
A door characterized by having glass panes throughout, or nearly throughout, its entire length; usually found in pairs.
Synonyms: **casement door, door window, French window**

French drain
A drainage trench filled with rock or brick fragments and covered with soil.
Synonyms: **boulder ditch, rubble drain**

fret
A geometrical design formed by a repeating series of interlocking angular lines.
Synonyms: **key pattern, Greek key**

frieze
In classical architecture, the member between the architrave and cornice. Also, any plain or decorative band, or board, on the top of a wall immediately below the cornice; sometimes decorated with festoons or other ornamentation. Porch cornices may likewise be decorated with friezes. A common example of such ornamentation, the **spindled porch frieze**, is illustrated.

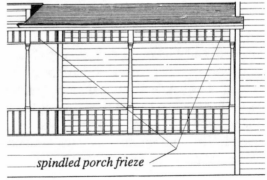

spindled porch frieze

furring

Strips of wood or metal that are attached to wall studs, ceiling joists, etc., so that a level surface is formed for finish material. Furring also can be attached to interior brick walls thereby creating an insulative and moisture preventive air space.

Synonyms: **furring strips**

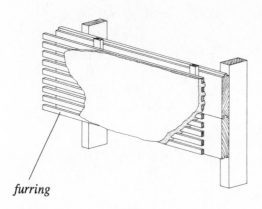

furring

gable

The triangular end of an exterior wall in a building with a ridged roof.

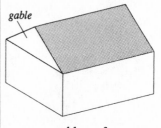

gable roof

gable roof

A sloping (ridged) roof that terminates at one or both ends in a gable.

Synonyms: **pitched roof, ridge roof, comb roof**

gablet

A small gable; frequently found over a dormer window or on the top of a roof.

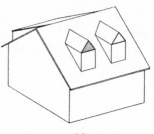

gablet

gable trim

The ornamental trim on the gable of a building; ranges from simple sawn wood or patterned shingle ornamentation to elaborate spindle work.

Synonyms: **gable ornament**

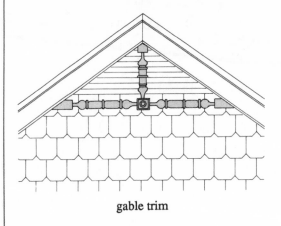

gable trim

gain

A notch cut in one member to receive the end of another member; notches may also be cut in both members.

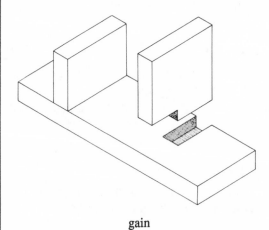

gain

gallery
A raised (i.e., above the first floor level) veranda or walkway running along the facade of a building; a long covered walk or passageway. Sometimes the term is used synonymously with porch and veranda.
Synonyms: **galerie**

galleting
The insertion of small stones or spalls into mortar joints for decorative, and possibly structural, purposes.

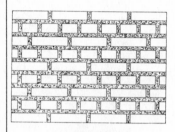
galleting

gambrel roof
A roof having a double slope on two sides of a building.
Synonyms: **mansard roof, gambrel**

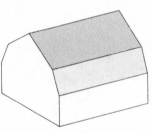
gambrel roof

garderobe
A clothes closet or wardrobe; a small private space, such as a bedroom.

garland
An ornament in the form of a band, a wreath, or a festoon of leaves, fruit, flowers, or oats.

garret
The space, usually with sloping walls, just below the roof; an attic.

gazebo
A small summerhouse or other space with a view; usually found in a garden or yard, but may also be incorporated into the facade of a building, or found on the roof of a house (in which case it is called a **belvedere**).

gazebo

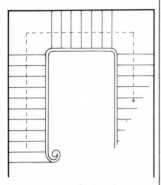

geometrical stair

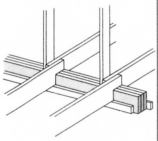

built-up girder

geometrical stair

A winding or angled stair having no newels at the turning points. See: open newel stair.

Georgian (1700 - 1780)

An architectural style characterized by: symmetry of floor plan and facade, usually gable or gambrel roof, central chimney, row of rectangular lights (panes) in or above the door, door flanked by columns or pilasters and capped by a decorative crown or a triangular pediment, and six-pane to twelve-pane double hung windows.

girder

A large or principal horizontal member of wood or metal used to support concentrated vertical loads. A wooden girder may be either a solid timber or a built-up member (in which case it is often called a **built-up girder** or a **built-up beam**).

girt

A horizontal beam that receives the ends of floor joists and summers in timber framing. See illustration on page 168.
Synonyms: **girth**

glass

Various types of plain and decorated glass are discussed below:

- **bent glass.** Glass formed by heating the mass to a plastic state and then allowing it to sag into a mold; all detail work must be done before the glass is heated.

- **beveled glass.** Glass in which edges are ground and polished to form a beveled border; used for entrance doors and other ornamental work.

- **brilliant cut.** After fogging a piece of glass by sandblasting or by using acid, a design is cut into the surface and subsequently polished so as to give off a "brilliant" luster.

- **chipped glass, glue chip glass.** Glass that exhibits an uneven, frosted appearance. It is manufactured by coating the surface with glue and then heating; heating causes the glue to chip off, each chip taking a sliver of glass with it.

- **cut glass.** Glass shaped or decorated through a process of grinding and polishing; the finished product often appears prismatic.

- **etched glass.** A decorative technique involves coating the glass surface with a *resist* material (such as beeswax), cutting a design into the coating, and then applying acid (which reacts only to the areas in which the resist material has been removed). Very fine details are possible through this technique.

- **flashed glass, cased glass, case glass.** A type of multi-layered glass in which at least one layer is either iridescent or colored.

- **plate glass**. A flat, transparent, relatively thin, high-grade glass with polished surfaces that have no blemishes and show no distortions. The manufacturing process involves casting and rolling sheets that are later ground and polished.

- **rolled figured glass, rolled and figured glass, figured rolled glass**. A flat glass in which vision is more or less obscured by patternwork. This type of glass is manufactured by rolling or impressing a decorative design in one surface of the sheet.

- **sandblasted glass, sand-blast glass**. Glass in which the surface is dulled to a smooth and milky finish through sandblasting; designs are possible by blasting sand over a stencil.

- **stained glass**. Colored glass used in mosaics and in windows.

- **window glass, sheet glass**. A flat, transparent, relatively thin glass having glossy fire finished surfaces that exhibit a characteristic waviness when viewed at an acute angle. The manufacturing process involves hand or machine blowing and drawing into sheets (or into cylinders that are then flattened).

- **wire glass**. Polished or figured glass with a core of wire mesh; used where security is a consideration.

glazing
Fitting glass into windows and doors.

Gothic Revival (1830 - 1880)
An architectural style characterized by: overall picturesque cottage or castle appearance, steeply pitched roof with cross gables, extensive use of ornamental bargeboards, hood molding over windows, doors and windows incorporating the Gothic arch, and the wall on the gable ends being uninterrupted.

grade
The point where the foundation wall or pier meets the surrounding fill.
Synonyms: **grade line**

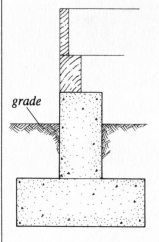

Greek Revival (1825 - 1860)
An architectural style characterized by: low-pitched gable (or sometimes hipped) roof, a frieze, a pedimented gable, a porch (or portico) with usually non-fluted columns, insignificant chimneys, elongated six-over-six double hung windows, a four panel door flanked by side lights with a transom window above, and bevel siding.

grille
A grating or openwork barrier used to cover, and often decorate, a wall or floor opening.

grotesque
Whimsical distortions of human and animal forms, either sculpted or painted (e.g., chimeras, griffins, goblins, basilisks, gargoyles, makharas, etc.).

grotesque

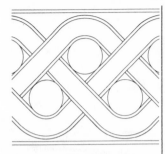

guilloche

guilloche
An ornament, used most frequently as an enrichment on molding, that resembles twisted bands; the spaces between bands are often filled with round elements.
Synonyms: **twisted rope**

gusset
A flat bracket used to stiffen the connection of two wood members; most often found at the joints of wood trusses.

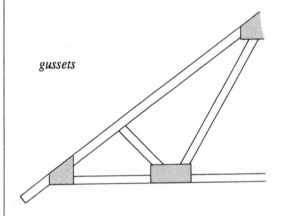

gussets

guttae
The small vertical elements found under the triglyphs or mutules on the Doric entablature. See illustration on page 15.
Synonyms: **drops**

gutter
A channel of wood or metal running along the eaves of a house; used for catching and carrying off rainwater and water from melting snow.
Synonyms: **eave trough**

gutter

gypsum lath
A sheet, usually measuring 16 inches by 48 inches, or 24 inches by 96 inches, having a gypsum core faced with paper on both sides and sometimes having round holes running through it; used as a base for plaster on interior walls.
Synonyms: **rock lath, sheetrock, gypsum board, board lath, gypsum plaster board, plaster board**

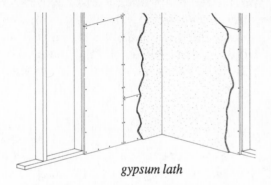

gypsum lath

half notch
A corner notch formed by removing the bottom half of a log or timber.
Synonyms: **halved-and-lapped notch, single notch**

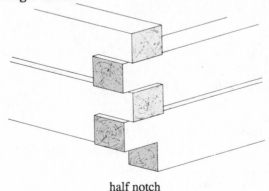

half notch

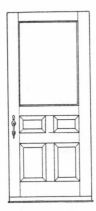

half-glass door

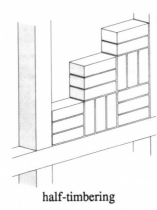

half-timbering

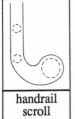
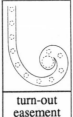

| handrail scroll | turn-out easement |

half-glass door
A door with glass panes above the middle (lock) rail.
Synonyms: **sash door**

half-timbering
A method of construction, common in sixteenth and seventeenth century England, in which the spaces between the vertical structural timbers were filled with brickwork or plaster. American derivatives of this method may be either structural or purely superficial. See: decorative half-timbering. In true half-timbering the plaster and brick infill is called **nogging**.

hall
A large room or corridor at the entrance of a building; commonly used for public gatherings and entertainment.
Synonyms: **entrance hall**

hall chamber
A private living space above the hall.

handrail
A railing that serves as a hand support along a stairway.
Synonyms: **top rail, rail**

handrail scroll/turn-out easement
A handrail scroll is a spiral turn at the end of a handrail; also called **scroll, handrail wreath, wreath, volute**. A turn-out easement

is a smaller version of a handrail scroll characterized by a simple turn out at the end of a handrail.

hanger
A metal strap attached to a wall or to a horizontal structural member and used to support a joist or beam.
Synonyms: **stirrup**

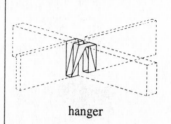

hanger

hatchway
An opening in the roof or floor of a building that is equipped with a hinged or removable cover.
Synonyms: **hatch**

haunch
That part of a structural member that lies beyond the shoulder and is received by another member (e.g., the uncut portion of the tenon that is carried by the mortise). Also, the portion of an arch between the crown (top) and the impost (side); the shoulder of an arch. See illustration on page 72.
Synonyms: **flank**

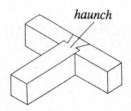

haunch

head
The prominent end of a member; the uppermost member of a structure; the top horizontal member over a door or window opening. See illustration on page 83.

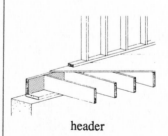

header

header
A door or window head. Also, the structural member that is nailed to the ends of the floor joists. A **double header** is used to frame out

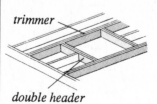

trimmer

double header

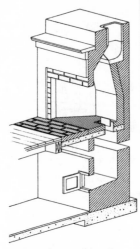

inner and outer hearths

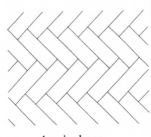

herringbone

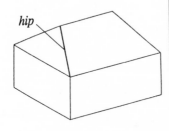

floor openings, or to frame out the top of door or window openings.

heading joint
A joint formed when two members are joined end-to-end.

hearth
The fire-resistant floor inside, and sometimes immediately in front of, a fireplace. Sometimes a distinction is made between the **inner hearth** (i.e., the portion within the fireplace) and the **outer hearth.**

heel
That part of a framing member which rests on the top plate.

herringbone
A pattern consisting of courses of obliquely oriented members, each course being aligned in the opposite direction from the ones above and below; most often found in brickwork and flooring.

hip
An external angle formed by the meeting of two sloping roof surfaces.

hip and valley roof
A roof constructed of both hips and valleys. Three common types of hip and valley roofs are the **cross gable,** the **offset gable,** and the **projecting gable.** See illustrations on the following page.

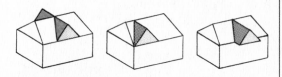

cross, offset, and projecting gables

hip gambrel roof
A combination of a hip roof and a gambrel roof.

hip roll
A rounded piece of tile, wood, or metal used to cover, finish, and sometimes add a decorative effect, to the ridge or hip of a roof.
Synonyms: **ridge roll**

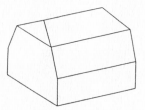

hip gambrel roof

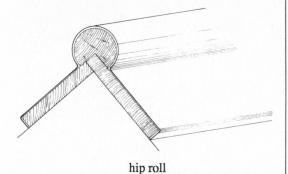

hip roll

hip roof
A roof formed by four pitched roof surfaces. Shown is a **hip roof with gablet** (also called **Dutch hip roof**).
Synonyms: **hipped roof**

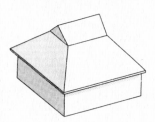

hip roof with gablet

hollow molding
A concave molding that forms more than a half circle; the opposite of roll molding.

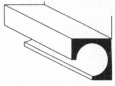

hollow molding

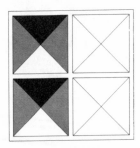

hollow square molding

hollow square molding
A molding consisting of a series of indented pyramids.

hood
A protective and sometimes decorative cover found over doors, windows, or other objects.
Synonyms: **hood molding**

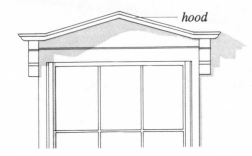

hood

hopper window
A window that is hinged either on both sides or on the bottom and swings inward.

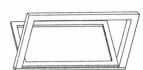

hopper window

housed joint
A joint formed when the full thickness of one member is inserted (housed) in another member, usually at right angles.
Synonyms: **dado joint**

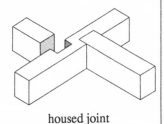

housed joint

imbrication
The weathertight covering formed by overlapping rows of plain or end-modified tiles or shingles thereby producing distinctive surface patterns. Illustrated are nine commonly seen wall and roof patterns: (A) diamond, (B) octagonal, (C) fish scale, (D) segmental, (E) cove, (F) hexagonal, (G) staggered, (H) square, and (I) wavy.

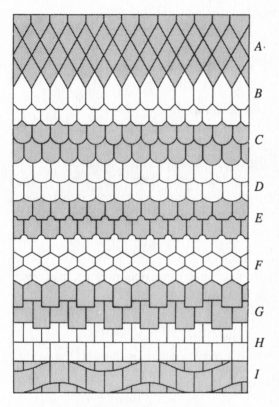

imbrication (see text)

impost
The horizontal block or other structural member that receives the end of an arch and distributes the thrust.

inglenook
A nook, or recessed space, adjacent to a fireplace, etc.; often contains shelves and seating.
Synonyms: **ingle recess, roofed ingle, chimney corner**

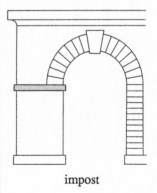

impost

inlaid work
A decorative field formed by inlaying or set-ting small pieces of material into a matrix of differing material.

International (1920 - 1945)
An architectural style characterized by: a flat roof, smooth stucco or plaster surfaces with little or no ornamentation, metal casement or sliding windows placed flush with the wall surface and having no decorative trim, and cantilevered balconies (in larger examples).

intrados
The innermost curve, or underside, of an arch. See illustration on page 72.

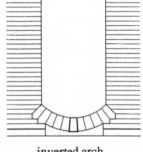

inverted arch

inverted arch
An arch in which the keystone is the lowest point.

Ionic order
A classical order characterized by a capital embellished with opposing volutes (spiral designs).

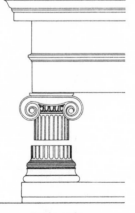

Ionic order

Italianate (1840 - 1880)
An architectural style characterized by: two or three stories, low-pitched hip (or some-times gable) roof with widely overhanging eaves supported by large brackets, a cupola or tower, visually balanced facades, decora-tive bracketed crowns or lintels over widows and doors, and narrow single pane double hung windows and double doors.

Italian Renaissance (1890 - 1930)
An architectural style characterized by: stone construction, low-pitched hip (or sometimes flat) roof with widely overhanging eaves supported by decorative brackets, ceramic tiled roof, round arches incorporated into doors and first story windows, and the frequent use of porticos or columned recessed entryways.

jerkinhead

jerkinhead
A roof form characterized by a clipped, or truncated, gable.
Synonyms: **jerkin, cupped gable, hipped gable, sheadhead**

joinery
The craft of connecting members together through the use of various types of joints; differs from carpentry in that the latter involves framing and rough work. Joinery is used extensively in trim work (e.g., doors, panels, etc.) and in cabinet work. Also, through an extension in its meaning, joinery refers to the connecting and securing of the structural members in framing, especially timber framing.

joint
In carpentry and woodworking, the place where two or more members meet.

jointing
The use of mortar as horizontal and vertical spacing between adjacent bricks. Seven common jointing types are illustrated: **flush** (also

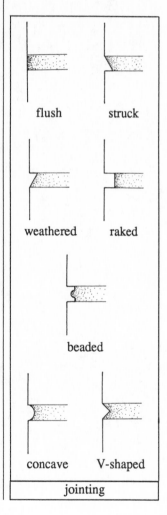

flush   struck

weathered   raked

beaded

concave   V-shaped

jointing

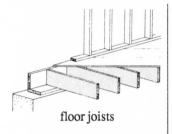
floor joists

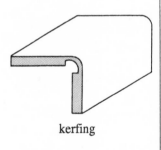
ceiling joists

kerfing

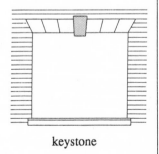
keystone

called **rain cut, plain,** and **smooth**), **struck, weathered** (or **weather**), **raked** (or **raked-out**), **beaded** (or **bead**), **concave** (or **rodded**), and **V-shaped.**

joists
Horizontal framing members that run parallel to each other from wall to wall. **Floor joists** provide a supporting framework for floors; **ceiling joists** provide a base for furring strips or plywood sheets.

keeping room
A living room.
Synonyms: **common room**

kerfing
The method of forming a corner or bend by cutting grooves across a board and then forming the board into the desired angle; probably most often found in stair construction.

keystone
The wedge-shaped stone found at the center of an arch.

kiss marks
Discolorations on the surface of bricks caused by the method of stacking before they are fired in a kiln. In more recent times, bricks with kiss marks have been used ornamentally.

lancet arch

A pointed arch composed of two curves with radii much larger than its span (width). See **pointed arch** for comparison.

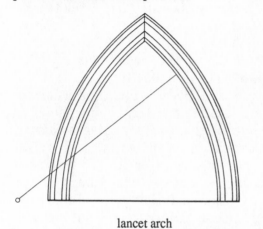

lancet arch

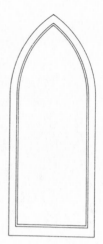

lancet window

lancet window

A long, narrow window with a pointed arch.

landing

A platform between flights of stairs; used to change directions of a stairway or to serve as a resting place. See **winder** for comparison.

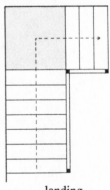

landing

lantern, cupola, belvedere

Although these terms are frequently used synonymously, distinctions may be made between the three (note the emphasis on key words):

- **lantern, lanthorn.** A *small* structure on a roof or dome with windows or openings *for the admittance of light.*

lantern

- **cupola**. A small *domed* structure crowning a roof or tower.

- **belvedere**. A rooftop gazebo, pavilion, or tower *for the sake of a view*.

lap joint

A joint composed of two overlapping members of equal size; usually formed by cutting away one-half the thickness of each member to be joined so that the resulting joint is on one plane. A lap joint formed on a corner is termed **end-lap joint**; one that is formed by the crossing of two members is called **cross-lap joint**; an end-to-end lap joint is referred to as a **splice**, or simply a **half-lap joint**. Sometimes the term **mid-lap joint** is used to refer to a lap joint formed when the end of one member intersects another member at a point other than its end.
Synonyms: **half-lap joint, halved joint, having joint**

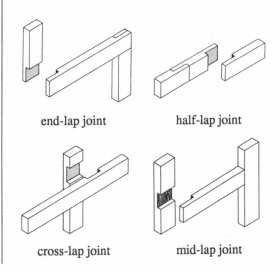

end-lap joint   half-lap joint

cross-lap joint   mid-lap joint

larder
A cool room used for the storage of meat and other food supplies.

lath
Wood strips, metal strips or channels, or gypsum board that are attached to framing members and are used as a supporting base for plaster, tiles, shingles, or other building materials.

lattice window
A window with diamond-shaped window panes.

latticework
Openwork produced by interlacing or crossing lath or thin strips of iron or wood. See: trellis.
Synonyms: **trellis work**

lattice window

latticework

leaded glass
Small panes of clear or stained glass that are held in position by means of lead strips.

leaf
A hinged part; one of the movable members of a door or shutter. Also, one of the two halves of a cavity wall. The term **valve** is sometimes used to describe one of the leaves of a French door, double door, etc. In the realm of architectural ornamentation, the term leaf is used to describe a decorative motif that represents a leaf; quite often applied to molding.

lean-to
A house that has a small addition with a lean-to (single-pitched) roof.
Synonyms: **lean-to house**

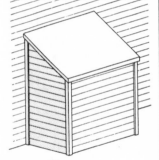

lean-to roof

lean-to roof
Usually refers to a single-pitch roof that is carried by a higher wall.
Synonyms: **half span roof**

ledger strip
A horizontal strip attached to girders or studs to carry floor joists. Ledger strip, ledger, and ledger board are usually used to describe strips attached to girders; whereas ribbon strip, ribbon board, and bearer are most often used to describe strips attached to studding.
Synonyms: **ribbon strip, ledger, ledger board, ribbon board, girt strip, bearer**

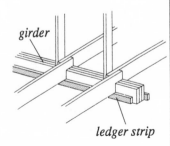

girder

ledger strip

lintel
A horizontal structural member that supports a load over an opening; usually made of wood, stone, or steel; may be exposed or obscured by wall covering. See illustration on page 83.

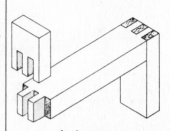

lock corner
A joint composed of interlocking fingers or pins. Sometimes a dovetail joint is classified as a type of lock corner, but for the sake of clarity these two terms should probably not be used synonymously.
Synonyms: **lock corner joint, box joint, finger joint, slip joint**

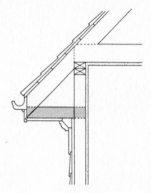

lock corner

loft
A space commonly found above the main floor in cabins and barns; used for sleeping or storage and usually accessed by way of a ladder; frequently open to the room below on one side.

lookout

lookouts
Short wooden brackets or cantilevers that support an overhanging portion of a roof. Also, short brackets for connecting the tails of rafters to the side of the house, thereby providing a nailing surface for the soffit.
Synonyms: **lookout rafters**

louver
A small lantern or other opening, often with wood slats, used for ventilating attics or other spaces.
Synonyms: **ventilator**

louver

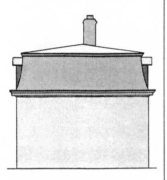
lozenge molding

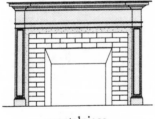
mansard roof

lozenge
A diamond-shaped decorative motif.

lozenge molding
A molding that incorporates lozenges as the major decorative theme.
Synonyms: **lozenge fret, diamond fret**

lunette
A semicircular opening that serves as decorative relief for the tympanum or other building surface. The term can also be applied to any flat semicircular surface, whether open or paneled.

mansard roof
A roof having two slopes on all four sides; the lower slope is much steeper than the upper.
Synonyms: **mansard**

mantel
Although this term generally refers to the ornamental work or facing around a fireplace (i.e., the mantelpiece), it is also often used synonymously with chimney bar and mantelshelf.

mantelpiece

mantelpiece
The fittings and ornamental embellishment surrounding a fireplace.
Synonyms: **chimneypiece**

mantelshelf
The part of the Mantelpiece that forms a shelf; sometimes supported by consoles. See illustration on page 76.

masonry
Work constructed by a mason using stone, brick, concrete blocks, tile, or similar materials.

masonry veneer
An outer covering laid against, but not structurally bonded to, a wall; used to cover inferior structural material thereby giving an improved appearance at a lower cost. Also, masonry veneer may be used as an alternative exterior siding for wood framed houses. **Brick veneer** (or **brick facing**), **stone veneer** (or more specifically **ashlar veneer**), and **cobblestone veneer** are illustrated.

metal ceiling
A ceiling covering constructed of stamped metal plates. Metal ceilings came in many patterns and colors, and were intended to imitate decorative plaster or wood ceilings; most often found in public (versus domestic) architecture.
Synonyms: **tin ceiling, metal coffering**

metope
The panel between the triglyphs in the Doric frieze; often treated in some decorative manner. See illustration on page 15.

Mission (1890 - 1920)
An architectural style characterized by stucco walls, round arches supported by piers, continuous wall surface forming parapets, hip roof with red tile roof covering, decorative stringcourse outlining the arches, and

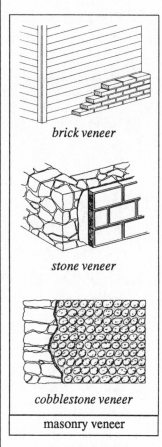

brick veneer

stone veneer

cobblestone veneer

masonry veneer

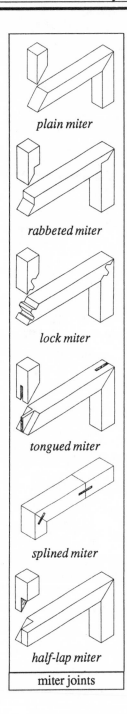

plain miter

rabbeted miter

lock miter

tongued miter

splined miter

half-lap miter

miter joints

overhanging eaves with exposed rafters. (Towers, curvilinear gables, and gablets found in larger examples of this style.)

miter
An angular shape formed by joining two obliquely cut members of similar size.

miter joint
A joint formed through the use of a miter. Besides the **plain miter joint** shown, this type of joint can take on many forms, largely through the combination of the plain miter with other basic joinery configurations. Some representative examples are given below:

- **rabbeted miter, ledge and miter, rabbeted ledge and miter**, formed through the combination of a miter and a rabbet (or ledge)

- **lock miter**, composed of a miter with interlocking edges

- **tongued miter**, composed of a miter with a spine-like tongue

- **splined miter**, formed through the combination of a miter and a spline (thin piece of wood)

- **half-lap miter**, formed through the combination of a miter and a half-lap

modillions
Ornamental blocks or brackets used in series to support the corona (overhang) in the composite or Corinthian orders.

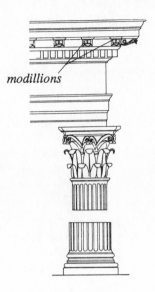

modillions

molding
A continuous decorative band; serves as an ornamental device on both the interior and exterior of a building or structure; also often serves the function of obscuring the joint formed when two surfaces meet. The eight basic molding types are: fillet, astragal (or bead), torus, ovolo, scotia, cavetto, cyma recta, and cyma reversa; all other molding types are generated from combinations or modifications of, or embellishments to, the eight types mentioned above.
Synonyms: **moulding**

mortar
A mixture of plaster, cement, or lime with a fine aggregate and water; used for pointing and bonding bricks or stones. A typical **lime mortar** consists of about one part slaked lime to six parts of sand.

mortise
A rectangular cavity cut in a member; receives a projecting part (the tenon, or tongue) from another member.
Synonyms: **pocket, housing**

mortise and tenon
A joint composed of a mortise (cavity) and a tenon (projection).

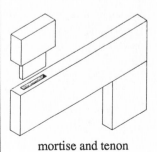

mortise and tenon

mosaic
A decorative field formed by inlaying small pieces of stone, glass, or other material into a matrix of mortar, plaster, or cement.
Synonyms: **mosaic work**

mudsill
A foundation timber placed directly on a patch of levelled earth or on flat stones. In early-American architecture this timber was often referred to as a **groundsill** or **grunsill**.

mullion
A large vertical member separating two casements; the vertical bar between coupled windows or multiple windows; the central vertical member of a double-door opening.
Synonyms: **munnion**

multiple roof
A roof consisting of a combination of roof forms. This roof type is a commonly seen feature on Queen Anne style houses.

muntin
One of the thin strips of wood used for holding panes of glass within a window; also called **munnion, bar, sash bar, glazing bar, window bar, division bar, munton bar**. Also, the central vertical member of a door; sometimes called a **mortant**. See illustration on page 133.

mutules
Ornamental blocks found above the triglyphs and below the corona in the Doric order.

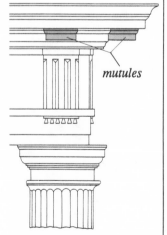

mullion

mutules

neck
The wide band between the shaft and the capital proper in the Doric and Tuscan orders. See illistration on page 15.
Synonyms: **necking**

newel
The post supporting the handrail at the top and bottom of a stairway. Intermediate newels are sometimes called **angle posts.** Newels are sometimes given names according to their location along a stairway (e.g., **starting newel, landing newel,** and so on). See illustration below.
Synonyms: **newel post**

newel cap
The crowning feature of a newel; often decorative in shape.

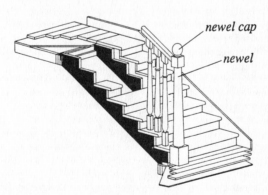

newel cap

newel

newel and newel cap

Neoclassical (1900 - 1940)
An architectural style characterized by: a two story pedimented portico or porch supported by colossal columns (usually with Ionic,

Corinthian, or composite capitals), a centrally located doorway, and symmetrically placed windows.

New England Colonial (1600 - 1700)
An architectural style characterized by: a box-like appearance, two stories with a centrally-located chimney, linear floor plan (i.e., one room deep), exterior wall covering of weatherboarding or shingles, small casement windows, steeply pitched gable roof with little or no overhang and no decorative treatment, and a simple batten door.

niche
A recess in a wall; may contain a piece of sculpture, etc.

nosing
The projecting rounded edge of a stair tread. The end of a tread that projects beyond the balusters in an open string stair is called a **return nosing**, or a **tread return**. See illustration on page 158.

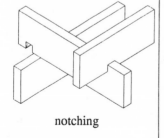
notching

notching
A method of securing crossing members to one another by cutting notches in one or both of the members (e.g., the notching at the corners of a cabin or timber structure).

nursery
A room or space set aside for small children and infants.

Octagon (1850 - 1870)
An architectural style characterized by: eight-sided shape, two or three stories, encircling veranda, a cupola or belvedere, and minimal exterior detailing (sometimes no more than decorative brackets).

on center
A means of indicating spacing by measuring from the center of one member to the center of the next member; 16" o.c. and 24" o.c. are the most commonly found joist, stud, and rafter spacings.
Synonyms: **o.c.**

open newel stair
A stair built around a wellhole. Note that, unlike the geometrical stair, newels are placed at the angles or turning points.
Synonyms: **hollow newel stair, open-well stair**

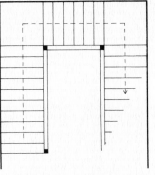
open newel stair

order
A style of column and its entablature (i.e., the section resting on the top of the column). In classical architecture, order refers to the specific configuration and proportions of the column including the base, shaft, capital, and entablature. See: composite order, Corinthian order, Doric order, Ionic order, and Tuscan order.

oriel window
A bay window located above the first floor level; usually supported by brackets or corbels.

oriel window

ornamental plasterwork

Carved or molded decorative plasterwork; such work may include moldings, panels, cornices, decorative ceilings, rosettes, or centerpieces. The terms **parget, pargetting, pergetting, pergeuring, parging**, and **parge work** refer more specifically to an ornamental facing for plaster walls; they likewise can refer to a coat of mortar applied to masonry walls.

ornaments

Details added to a structure solely for decorative reasons (i.e., to add shape, texture, or color to an architectural composition).

outbuilding

An auxiliary structure that is located away from a house or principal building (e.g., a root cellar, a spring house, a smoke house, a corn crib, etc.).

outlet ventilator

A louvered opening in the gable end of a building that provides ventilation.

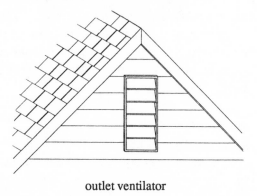

outlet ventilator

outshot
A small extension or wing built against an exterior wall of a house.
Synonyms: **outshut**

overhang
The projection of one story beyond the one below. Also, the part of the roof that extends beyond the wall plane.
Synonyms: **jetty**

overmantel
A panel, mirror, or the like, placed above the mantelshelf.

ovolo
A wide convex molding; also referred to as **quarter round** or **quatro round**.
Synonyms: **ovolo molding**

ovolo

Palladian window
A window composed of a central arched sash flanked on either side by smaller side lights.
Synonyms: **Venetian window**

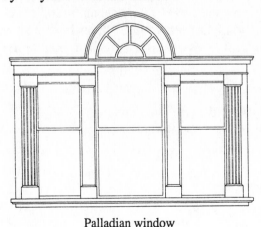

Palladian window

six-over-six double
hung window

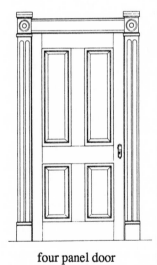

four panel door

pane
A single piece of window glass. Windows are often described according to the number of panes they have. For example, a window with eight panes of glass is called an *eight light window*. Often a double hung window is described in terms of the number of panes in each of its two sashes (e.g., a *six-over-six double hung window* indicates that each sash has six panes).
Synonyms: **light, window pane, window light**

panel
A sunken or raised portion of a wall, ceiling, mantel, or door with a frame-like border.

paneled door
A door with one or more recessed panels. Paneled doors are given specific names according to the number of panels they possess (e.g., the *four panel door* illustrated at left), or according to the configuration of the panels (e.g., the *cross and bible door*). Oftentimes these two methods of classification overlap, as seen with the door illustrated on page 42, which could be called either a *five panel door* or a *horizontal panel door*.

paneling
A wall or ceiling decoration made up of a series of panels.

pantry
A storage room for bread, dry provisions, and other food supplies; a room between kitchen

and dining room used for serving food and beverages; a room used for the storage and/or distribution of beverages; a **buttery**; a **larder**.

parapet
A low wall or protective railing; often used around a balcony or balconet, or along the edge of a roof. See illustration of coping on page 54.

parlor
A room used principally for the entertainment of guests.
Synonyms: **sitting room**

parlor chamber
A private living space above the parlor.

parquetry
The decorative system where geometrical pieces of wood or stone are formed into predominantly geometrical patterns; usually at least two colors or two types of material are used. Parquetry is used in flooring, in wall construction, and in wainscotting.

parting strip
A vertical strip of wood used to separate the sashes of a window.

partition
An interior wall that separates adjacent rooms within any story of a building. **Bearing partitions** carry loads in addition to their own weight; whereas **nonbearing** (or **non load-**

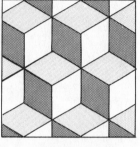

parquetry

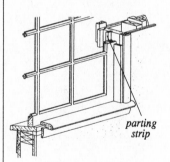

parting strip

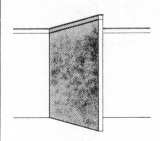

partition

bearing) **partitions** act only as dividing walls and do not support vertical loads.

passageway
A space serving as a thoroughfare, or as a means of connecting one room or area to another in a building; a **corridor** or **gallery**. Synonyms: **passage**

patera

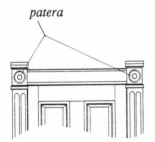

patera
(pl. **paterae**) A small round or oval disk or medallion; may be quite simple, such as the **corner block paterae** illustrated, or richly adorned with representations of leaves, flowers, and other decorative devices. Synonyms: **button**

patio
A usually paved and shaded area adjoining or enclosed by the walls of a house; used for outdoor living or entertainment.

patterned brickwork
Brickwork formed into various patterns through the use of bricks of two or more colors or textures. **Dichromatic brickwork** refers specifically to the use of bricks of two colors to build up a pattern on walls, arches, corners, and around doors and windows. The use of more than two colors is termed **polychromatic brickwork**.

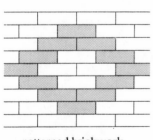

patterned brickwork

pavilion
A structure that is usually detached from the principal building and is used for entertainment or as a summer house. Also, a project-

ing element on an exterior wall, usually at the center or at each end of a building, that suggests a tower, or the like.

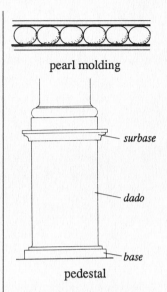
pearl molding

pearl molding
A molding consisting of a series of pearl-like elements.
Synonyms: **beading**

pedestal
In classical architecture, the molded block that supports a column or colonnade; consists of **base** (or **plinth**), **dado** (or **die**), and **surbase**. The term is used in a looser sense to describe the base for a statue or other superimposed architectural feature.

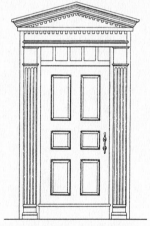
surbase

dado

base

pedestal

pediment
A triangular section framed by a horizontal molding on its base and two raking (sloping) moldings on each of its sides; used as a crowning element for doors, windows, overmantels, and niches. A **pedimented entrance door** and a **pedimented window hood** are illustrated. Pediments with discontinuous framing members can generally be broken down into the following categories:

- **broken apex pediment, open topped pediment.** A pediment where the two sloping sides do not meet at the apex (top) of the pediment.

- **open bed pediment, broken bed pediment.** A pediment in which the base molding is discontinuous.

pedimented entrance door

pedimented window hood

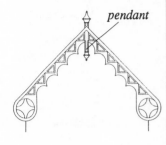

pendant

pendant
A hanging ornament; usually found projecting from the bottom of a construction member such as a newel in a staircase, the bottom of a bargeboard, or the underside of a wall overhang.
Synonyms: **pendent**

pier
One of the square pillars supporting an arch; the solid mass between two openings in a building. See illustration of pillars on the following page.

piers, pilings
Vertical supporting members that are part of the foundation. Three pier support systems commonly found in a building without a basement are discussed here. The first of these is a **pier foundation**, consisting of piers resting on footings and supporting grade beams (upon which the superstructure is built). In a **post and pier foundation**, illustrated at left, rows of wood and concrete piers, spaced at appropriate intervals, support beams which form a base for the superstructure. **Pilings**, made of timber, steel, or concrete, are often used where a structure is built on marshy ground. Each **pile** is driven deep into a stable stratum of earth. (See illustration on page 80.) Besides the three methods just mentioned, a basementless building may be supported by shallow foundation walls supported by footings. In such a case, posts and piers often are used for intermediate support underneath the building.

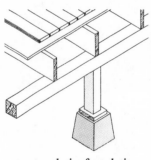

post and pier foundation

pilaster

A rectangular column or shallow pier attached to a wall; quite frequently decoratively treated so as to represent a classical column with a base, shaft, and capital.

pillars

Upright members primarily used for supporting superstructures; distinguished from columns in that pillars need not be cylindrical or conform to the measures of classically-inspired columns. Square pillars are often called **piers**.

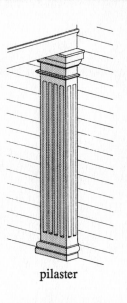

pilaster

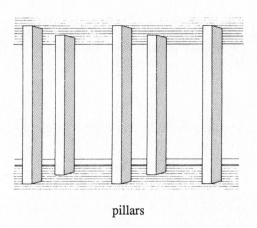

pillars

pin

A hardwood dowel used as a means of securing structural members together. The term **pin** is usually reserved for dowels with a diameter of less than 5/8", **peg** for dowels with a diameter ranging from 5/8" to 1 1/2", and **trenail** for dowels with a diameter of greater that 1 1/2" (usually about 2").

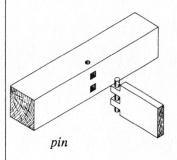

pin

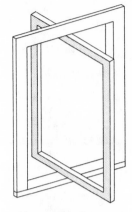

pivoted window

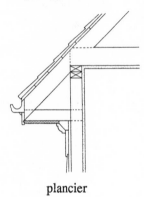

plancier

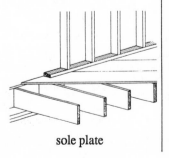

sole plate

pisé
Earth or clay rammed into a form until it becomes firm; used for walls and floors.

pivoted window
A window whose sash rotates on centrally located pivots.
Synonyms: **pivoted casement**

plancier
The exposed underside of any projecting member, such as a box cornice; a **soffit**.
Synonyms: **plancer, plancher, placeer**

planks
Long heavy pieces of timber; generally refers to all boards that are more than one inch thick and six or more inches wide.

plaster
A mixture of lime, gypsum, or portland cement with sand and water; applied in a plastic state to walls, ceilings, etc. Sometimes hair or other fibrous materials are added to the mixture as a binder.

plaster base
The surface to which plaster is applied; this surface may be wood lath, gypsum lath, metal lath, wire lath, wire fabric, fiberboard lath, masonry block, or brick.

plates
Horizontal pieces of timber in a wall used to support rafters, ceiling joists, and other structural members. The **sole plate** is the bottom

horizontal member of a frame wall; a **top plate** (or **wall plate**) is the horizontal member of a frame wall to which rafters or upper floor joists are fastened; the **sill plate** is a horizontal member anchored to a masonry wall.

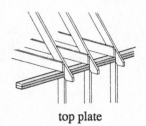

top plate

platform framing

A system of framing a building in which studs extend only one story at a time, and the floor joists of each story rest on the top plates of the story below, or on the sill for the first story.

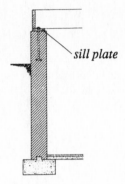

sill plate

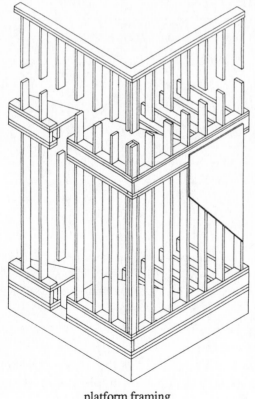

platform framing

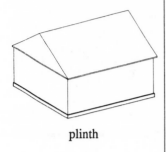

plinth

plinth
The base courses on an external wall when such courses give the appearance of a platform. Also, the square base for a column. See illustration on page 15.

plinth block
A small, slightly projecting block at the bottom of the door trim.

pointed arch
An arch composed of two curves with radii equal to its span (width). See **lancet arch** for comparison.
Synonyms: **equilateral arch**

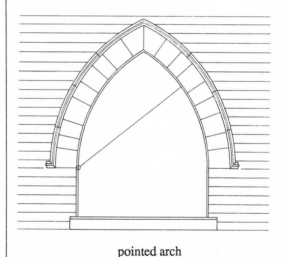

pointed arch

pointing
The treatment of masonry joints by filling with a high quality mortar; used to protect against the weather or simply to improve the appearance of a masonry wall.

porch
A covered entrance or semienclosed space projecting from the facade of a building; may be open sided, screened, or glass enclosed. Synonyms: **stoop**

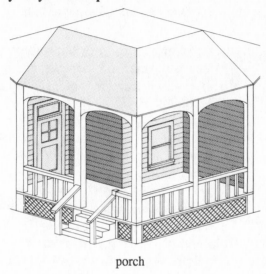

porch

porte-cochere
A covered entrance, or porch, projecting far enough across a driveway or entrance road so that automobiles, carriages, or other wheeled vehicles may easily pass through.

portico
A covered walk or porch supported by columns or pillars; a **colonnaded porch**.

portland cement
A hydraulic cement binder for concrete; made by burning a mixture of clay and limestone.

portico

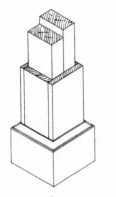

cased post

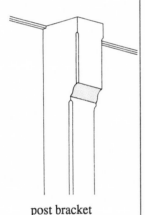

post bracket

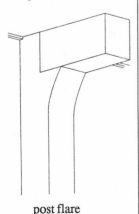

post flare

post

Any stiff, vertical, isolated upright made of wood, stone, or metal; used to support a superstructure or to afford a firm point for lateral attachment (such as for a gate). A few specific types of posts are discussed below:

- **corner post.** A solid or built-up post placed at a corner; a corner post in timber frame construction is often called a **principal post.**

- **prick post.** An intermediate or secondary post (such as the **chimney post** in timber frame construction).

- **puncheon.** A short post; a split log with a smoothed face; one of a series of closely spaced short posts upon which a building rests.

- **cased post.** A post faced with boards.

post bracket

A projection at the top of a post.

post flare

The tapering of a post; may take place just at the top or over the entire length of the post.

Prairie (1900 - 1920)

An architectural style characterized by its overall horizontal appearance (which is accomplished through the use of bands of casement windows, long terraces or balconies, flanking wings, low pitched roofs with wide overhangs, and darkly colored strips or bands on exterior walls).

Pueblo Revival (1905 - pres.)
A predominantly Southwestern architectural style characterized by: flat roofs with projecting rounded roof beams (called **vegas**); stucco covered battered walls with rounded corners; multi-paned, straight-headed windows set deeply into walls; and stepped or terraced upper stories.
Synonyms: **Spanish-Pueblo Revival**

purlins
Horizontal members in the roof frame that run on the top of, or between, rafters. See illustration on page 168.

pyramidal hipped roof
A pyramid-shaped roof with four sides of equal slope and shape.
Synonyms: **pyramidal roof**

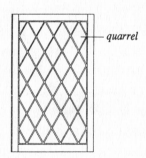

pyramidal hipped roof

quarrel
A small rectangular, triangular, or diamond-shaped pane of glass. The term also applies to small quadrangular openings in window tracery.
Synonyms: **quarry**

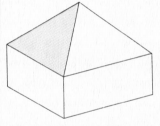

quarrel

Queen Anne (1880 - 1910)
An architectural style characterized by: irregularity of plan and massing, variety of color and texture, variety of window treatment, multiple steep roofs, porches with decorative gables, frequent use of bay win-

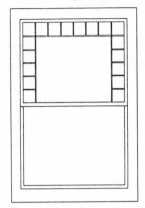

Queen Anne sash

dows, chimneys that incorporate molded brick or corbelling, and wall surfaces that vary in texture and material used.

Queen Anne sash
A window sash with many small geometrically shaped panes running along its edges; popular in the late-1800s and early-1900s.
Synonyms: **Queen Anne window**

quirk
A small V-shaped indentation that separates one architectural element from another; often found between moldings. Shown are a cyma reversa without a quirk and a cyma reversa with a quirk.

quirk

quirk bead
A bead with a quirk on one side; may be found along the lower exposed edge of horizontal wood siding, etc.
Synonyms: **quirked bead, bead and quirk**

quirk bead

quirked molding
A molding that has a small, sharply incised groove; the term is sometimes used to refer to a molding that is characterized by a convex and a concave curve separated by a flat portion.
Synonyms: **quirk molding**

quoins

Large stones, or rectangular pieces of wood or brick, used to decorate and accentuate the corners of a building; laid in vertical series with, usually, alternately large and small blocks. Besides their decorative purpose, some quoins actually serve the more functional purpose of reinforcing the corners of a building.

Synonyms: **coins, coin-stones**

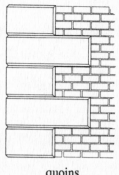

quoins

rabbet

A joint formed by cutting a rectangular groove in one member to receive the end of another member.

Synonyms: **rabbet joint, rabbeted joint, rebate**

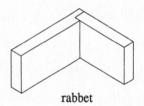

rabbet

rafters

The sloping members of a roof upon which a roof covering is placed. Rafters are given specific names largely according to their location and use. The major types are discussed and illustrated below:

- **common rafter**. A rafter that extends from the ridge beam or ridge board to the top plate.

- **hip rafter**. A rafter that forms the hip of a roof.

- **valley rafter**. A rafter that forms the valley of a roof.

- **jack rafter** (or **cripple rafter**). A short rafter in which one end terminates at

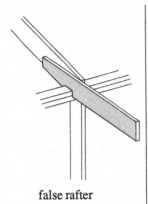

false rafter

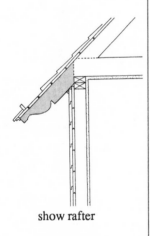

show rafter

rafter tail

either the hip or the valley of a roof (the former is sometimes called a **hip jack**, the latter a **valley jack**).

- **principal rafter.** One of the sloping members of a roof truss that provides support for the purlins upon which the common rafters rest. See illustration on page 173.

- **false rafter.** A short extension to a rafter; used for its visual effect or where the continuation of the roof slope to the overhang would be unacceptable.

- **show rafter.** A rafter which may be seen below the cornice; often decoratively treated.

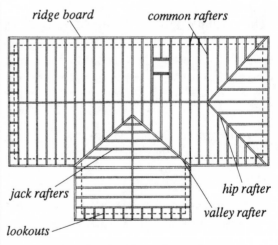

roof plan showing the various rafter types

rafter tail
The part of a rafter that projects beyond the wall.

rail

A horizontal member of a door or window. On a door, the uppermost member is called the **top rail**, the middle member the **lock rail**, and the lowest member the **bottom rail**. The bar that separates the upper and lower sash on a window is called the **meeting rail**. Sometimes the middle section of a double hung window, where the bottom rail of the upper sash meets the top rail of the lower sash, is called the **check rail**.

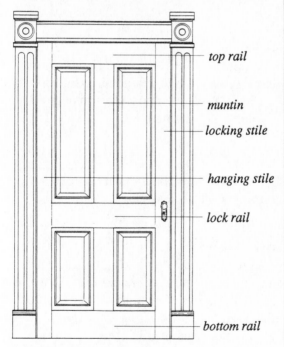

top rail

muntin

locking stile

hanging stile

lock rail

bottom rail

the members of a panel door

rainwater head

The enlargement near the top of a downspout; sometimes treated decoratively.
Synonyms: **leader head, conductor head**

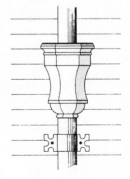

rainwater head

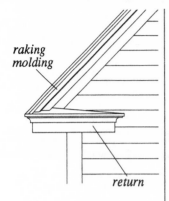

raking molding

return

rake
The slope of a gable, pediment, stair string, etc. The term is also used to describe any sort of trim that forms the finish between a wall and a sloping roof.

raking molding
Molding that follow the slope (rake) of a gable, pediment, etc.
Synonyms: **raked molding, molded rake board**

ramp
The upward concave turn in a handrail; used to bring an ascending handrail to the level of the rail above. See illustration on page 69.
Synonyms: **gooseneck**

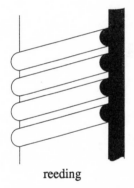

reeding

reeding
A molding consisting of parallel convex or semicylindrical elements.

relieving arch
An arch embedded in a wall; used to relieve the section below it of weight from above. A relieving arch is often found over a lintel or a flat arch.
Synonyms: **discharging arch**

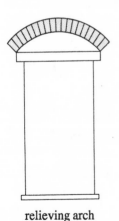

relieving arch

repoussé
Ornamental metal relief work produced by hammering metal into a form from the reverse side.
Synonyms: **repoussé work**

resilient flooring

A term used to describe smooth-surfaced floor coverings that exhibit similarities in manufacture and installation; became quite popular after about 1920. Four common types of resilient flooring are discussed below:

- **asphalt tile.** Low cost tile, usually nine inch squares, made from asphalt, asbestos fibers, mineral pigments, and ground limestone or other inert fillers; laid over a wood or concrete subfloor.

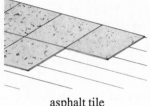
asphalt tile

- **linoleum.** The oldest form of resilient flooring, linoleum consists of canvas covered with hardened linseed oil and a filler (such as powdered cork); it may be plain, printed, or stamped with an oil paint, or inlaid with small pieces of colored linoleum; purchased in rolls or in tile form. Linoleum is usually laid on a saturated felt paper.

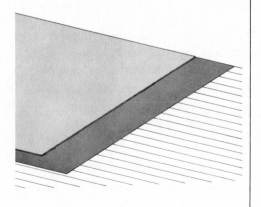
linoleum

- **rubber tile**. Rolls or tiles made of pure rubber combined with color pigments and powdered cork, cotton fibers, or other fillers; this soft and durable flooring is found most often in halls and kitchens.

- **cork tile**. A flooring tile mainly composed of granulated bark of the cork oak tree and synthetic resins; laid over either a wood or concrete subfloor.

retaining wall
A braced or freestanding wall that bears against an earthen backing.

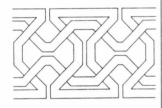

reticulated molding

reticulated molding
A molding covered with a network of interlacing lines; these lines may take the form of fillets or semicircular bands. (In the latter case the molding is sometimes referred to as **twisted rope**.)

return
The continuation of a molding from one surface onto an adjacent surface. A commonly encountered return is the **cornice return**, where the cornice is carried a short distance onto the gable end of a building. See illustration on page 134.

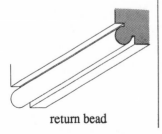

return bead

return bead
A molding consisting of a bead running along a corner or edge that is flanked on both sides by quirks or square indentations.

reveal
The vertical retreating surface of a window or door between the frame and the front of the wall.
Synonyms: **revel**

Richardsonian Romanesque (1880 - 1900)
An architectural style characterized by: round arches over door and window openings, a heaviness of appearance created by rock-faced stonework and deep window reveals, an asymmetrical facade, towers with conical roofs, porches with broad round arches supported by squat piers, and steep-gabled wall dormers.

reveal

ridge
The horizontal line formed when two roof surfaces meet.

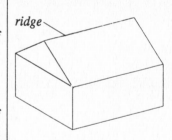

ridge beam/board/pole
The topmost horizontal member of a roof frame into which rafters are connected. The difference between a ridge beam, ridge board, and ridge pole lies in the size and shape of the member: a **ridge beam** is a heavy timber, a **ridge board** is a plank or board, and a **ridge pole** is a long log or pole (frequently found in cabin construction). See illustrations on pages 50 and 132.

ridge cap
A wood, metal, or shingle covering that caps the ridge of a roof.
Synonyms: **ridge capping, ridge covering**

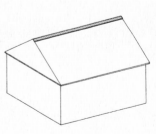

ridge cap

rinceau

rinceau
An ornamental motif consisting of inter-twined foliage.

riprap
Large pieces of irregularly-shaped quarry stone used for foundations and retaining walls.

riser
The vertical board under the tread, i.e., the front of a step. See illustration on page 158.

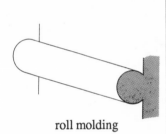

roll molding

roll molding
A convex molding that is semicircular or greater in section; the opposite of hollow molding.
Synonyms: **edge roll, bowtell**

roof covering
The protective, and sometimes decorative, covering that forms the exposed surface of a roof. Building materials that have been used as roof coverings in North American architecture include: bark, sod, thatch, board, copper, zinc, lead, tinplate, galvanized iron, ceramic tile, tar and gravel, wood shakes, slate, asbestos, wood shingles, asphalt shingles, metal shingles, and asphalt prepared (roll) roofing. Some of the more commonly seen roof coverings on domestic architecture are discussed below:

- **asbestos shingles.** Stiff, durable shingles made of asbestos fiber and portland cement combined under pressure; found in various colors and sizes.

- **asphalt shingles** (or **composition shingles, strip slates**). Shingles made of heavy asbestos or rag roofing felt saturated with asphalt and coated with mineral granules on the surface exposed to the weather.

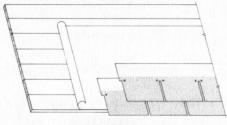

asphalt shingles

- **built-up roofing** (or **composition roofing, felt and gravel roofing, membrane roofing, gravel roofing**). A roof covering made up of layers of saturated felt, cloth, or paper; each layer is coated with a tar-like substance (e.g., asphalt, pine pitch, tar, coal tar, etc.); the roof is usually finished off with a coat of sand or gravel. Built-up roofing is usually restricted to buildings with low-pitched or flat roofs.

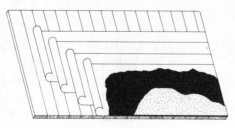

built-up roofing

- **metal roofing** (or **sheet metal roofing, tin roofing, sheet iron roofing**). Metal roofing made of tin-plate, terne-plate, copper, zinc, lead, or galvanized iron. Metal roofs, especially tin-plate, terne-plate, and galvanized iron, have been widely used in the United States since the mid-1800s. **Tin-plate** is made of sheet steel dipped in molten tin; whereas **terne-plate** is made by dipping sheet steel in a bath of molten tin and lead. Unlike tin-plate, **galvanized iron**, which is coated with a layer of zinc, is resistant to rust and therefore does not require painting. A popular style of galvanized roofing still being used today is **corrugated steel roofing**.

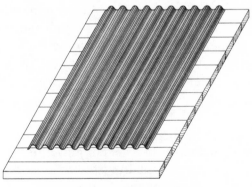

corrugated steel roofing

- **metal shingles**. Shingles made of sheet metal that is usually galvanized (coated with zinc), tin-plated (coated with tin), or terne-plated (coated with tin and lead); manufactured either singly or in sheets of four and found in a variety of patterns.

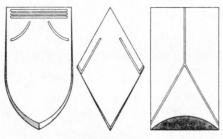

metal shingles

- **prepared roofing** (or **roll roofing, rolled roofing, ready roofing, asphalt prepared roofing, cold-process roofing, rolled strip roofing**). A roofing material made of asphalt-saturated felt covered by a layer of harder asphalt mixed with asbestos, mineral powder, glass fiber, or other materials; the surface exposed to the weather is often covered with mineral granules of various colors; comes in rolls.

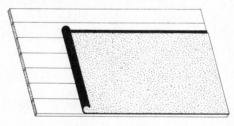

prepared roofing

- **roofing tile**. A building material made of fired clay, concrete, or asbestos cement; available in many configurations and types. Shown on the following page are eight commonly encountered tile types: **Spanish, pantile, mission, Roman, plain, English, Greek,** and **French**.

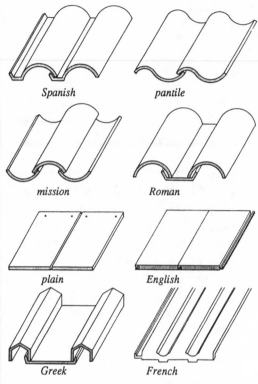

Spanish   *pantile*

mission   *Roman*

plain   *English*

Greek   *French*

eight types of roofing tile

- **shakes** (or **wood shakes**). Handcut wood shingles. Shakes can be distinguished from shingles in that shakes are not tapered and usually have more irregular surfaces. Their length varies from 12 inches to over three feet.

- **shingles**. Thin rectangular pieces of wood or other material used in overlapping rows as a means of covering walls or roofs; the butt of the shingles can be cut in a variety of shapes to give the shingled surface a distinctive pattern.

- **slate shingles**. Flat roofing shingles made of slate. Although slate shingles were heavy and usually more expensive than most roof coverings, they were extensively used because of their fire resistant qualities. Slate roofing also lends itself well to a variety of decorative patterns.

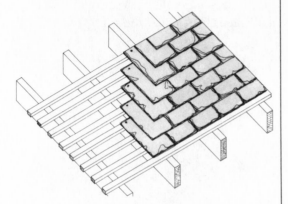

slate shingles

- **wood shingles**. A consistently popular roofing material in the United States, wood shingles take the form of thin, long pieces of wood that taper from one end to the other. Shingles, up until about 1850, were cut by hand; after this date sawing became the dominant means of manufacture. Wood shingles come dimensioned or in random widths, plain or end-modified; length is most often 16, 18, or 24 inches.

rosette

Any round ornament that is carved, painted, or molded so as to resemble a flower; used as

rosette

ornamental nailheads or screwheads, as decorative plaques in joinery, or simply as a means of embellishing a wall or ceiling. Paterae are often decorated with rosettes.
Synonyms: **rozette, rose**

roughly squared masonry
Masonry constructed of roughly squared and dressed stones; less accurately dressed (finished) than ashlar masonry.

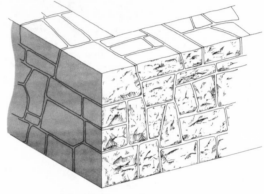

roughly squared masonry

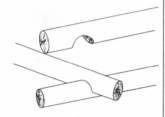

round notch

round notch
A corner notch formed by cutting a round depression in either the top or bottom of a log near its end. Related term: saddle notch.
Synonyms: **saddle notch, single saddle notch**

coursed rubble

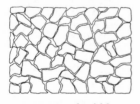

uncoursed rubble

rubblework
Masonry built of rubble or roughly quarried ˙ stones; used for crude walls or as backing for face stones. Uncoursed rubble masonry is sometimes called **cobweb rubble, random rubble, random work,** or **mosaic**.
Synonyms: **rubble masonry**

rustic work
"Decoration by means of rough woodwork, the bark being left in place, or by means of uncut stones, artificial rockwork, or the like, or by such combination of these materials and devices as will cause the general appearance of what is thought to be rural in character. Where woodwork is used it is customary to provide a continuous sheathing as of boards, upon which are nailed the small logs and branches with their bark, moss, etc., carefully preserved; but these strips of wood are often arranged in ornamental patterns, causing anything but a rural appearance" (Sturgis 1901-1902:392-398).

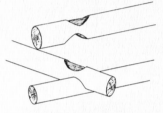

saddle notch
A type of corner notching characterized by a round or saddle-shaped depression on one side and a round (and often more shallow) depression on the other side.
Synonyms: **double saddle notch**

saddle notch

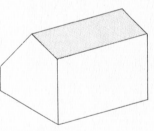

saltbox
A house design characterized by a roof with a short slope in front and a long slope, which sweeps close to the ground, in back. Sometimes called a **catslide**.
Synonyms: **saltbox house**

saltbox

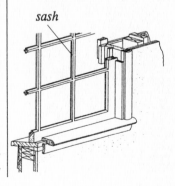

sash

sash
The framework into which panes are set.

sawn wood ornament
An ornament made with a jigsaw, band saw, or scroll saw; often served as a cheap sub-

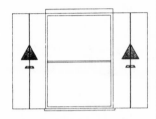

cut-out sawn-wood
ornament

stitute for carved and turned wood ornamentation. **Gingerbread,** characteristic of the romantic movement that swept United States architecture in the late-nineteenth century and early-twentieth century, takes the form of curves, scrolls, and lace-work on bargeboards, door and window trim, etc. See bargeboard illustration on page 24. The term **cut-out** usually refers to a simpler form of sawn wood ornamentation consisting of various decorative motifs (e.g., slots, squares, diamonds, plant forms) that are made by the use of the drill and keyhole saw. **Pierced work** is sometimes used to refer to wood ornaments that consist mainly or entirely of perforations.
Synonyms: **jigsaw ornament**

scab
A short piece of lumber used to strengthen a joint. Scabs may be bolted, nailed, or screwed to the larger abutting members.

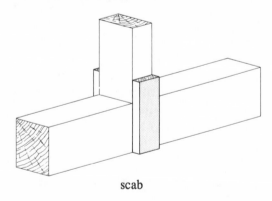

scab

scallop

scallop
A carved or molded ornament in the form of a series of curves resembling shells or seg-

ments of a circle; used on moldings, strips of wood, etc.

scantling

A piece of lumber of comparatively small cross-section (e.g., a 2x3 or 2x4) used for studding, roofing, or flooring. Another, more obscure, meaning for the word is a measure or standard for determining the dimensions of a piece of timber.

scarf joint

A joint formed by notching and lapping the ends of two members; a joint so formed is secured by various means: wedges, pegs, bolts, straps, or by the use of fishplates. **Scarf**, and **splice** are often used synonymously with this term. A few common scarf joints are discussed below:

- **true scarf joint**, consists of one or more angular cuts at the ends of the joining members

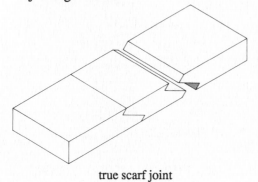

true scarf joint

- **half-lap scarf** (or **half-lapped scarf**), incorporates a half-lap joint.

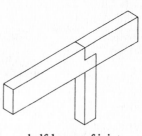

half-lap scarf joint

- **tabled scarf** (or **halved splice with wedges**), consists of "tabled" joining surfaces tightly secured through the use of wooden wedges

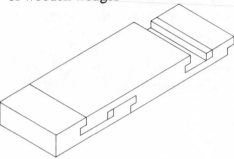

tabled scarf joint

- **beveled scarf** (or **beveled joint with wedges**), where joining surfaces are beveled and sometimes wedged

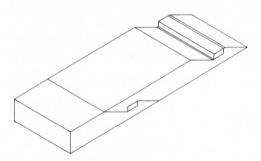

beveled scarf joint

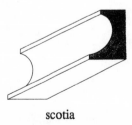

scotia

scotia
A concave molding, so named because of the dark shadow it casts. (Scotia means "dark one" in classical mythology).
Synonyms: **trochilus**

screen
A barrier whose function is to separate or conceal, but not to support; almost always treated decoratively in some way.

screen door
A door intended to allow ventilation but exclude insects; usually consists of a lightweight frame and fine wire mesh screening.

scroll molding
A molding that resembles a scroll with the free end hanging down; often used where a drip is needed, such as on a stringcourse.

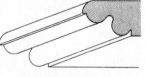

scroll molding

scrollwork
Any kind of ornamental work that is scroll-like in character.

scuttle
A hatchway or opening, equipped with a cover, and located in the ceiling.

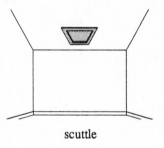

scuttle

Second Empire (1855 - 1890)
An architectural style characterized by: two or three stories, mansard (double-pitched) roof with multicolored slate shingles or metal shingles and dormer windows, pedimented and bracketed slender windows, ornate moldings and brackets (especially under the eaves), arched double doors, and, oftentimes, porches or projecting pavillions.

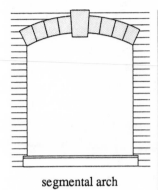

segmental arch

semicircular arch

segmental arch
An arch formed by an arc or by the segment of a circle.

semicircular arch
An arch in the form of a half circle.
Synonyms: **round arch, circular arch**

semilunate notch
Descriptive of the type of corner notching applied to half-round log construction or to the milled lumber that simulates half-round log construction.

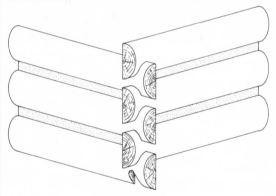

semilunate notch

shaft
The section of a column found between the base and capital. See illustration on page 15.

shale
A sedimentary rock, formed from clay or silt, that readily splits into layers; used as a roofing material because of its fire resistance and durability.

sheathing
Diagonal, horizontal, or spaced boards; plywood; or other material nailed to wall studding or roof rafters as a base for the finished siding or the roof covering.
Synonyms: **sheeting, tinning**

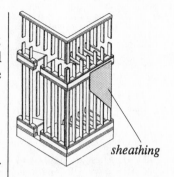

sheathing

shed roof
A roof consisting of one inclined plane. Unlike a lean-to roof, a shed roof need not be carried by a higher wall (i.e., it may serve as the primary roof form for a building).
Synonyms: **pent roof**

shell
A decorative motif that is a realistic representation of a shell. Related term: scallop.

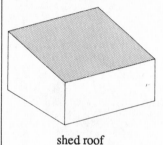

shed roof

Shingle (1880 - 1915)
An architectural style characterized by: uniform wall covering of wood shingles, hip or gable roofs with dormer windows, irregular roof line, small-paned windows, no corner boards, and a generally toned down appearance from that found with the Queen Anne style.

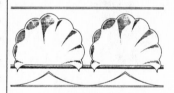

shell

shouldered housed joint
A joint formed when the full thickness of the end of one member is carried by the housing of the receiving member.

shutters
Solid blinds on either side of a window; may be plain or decorated, operative or purely ornamental, and on the inside or outside of a

shutters

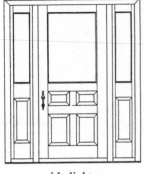

side lights

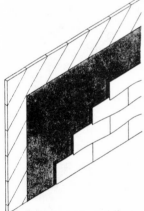

asbestos-cement siding

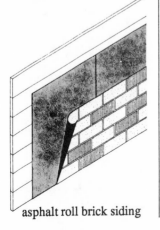

asphalt roll brick siding

building. Inside shutters are sometimes fitted into pockets called **shutter boxes.**

side light
A usually long fixed sash located beside a door or window; often found in pairs.
Synonyms: **winglight, flanking window, margin light**

siding, cladding
Although the term **siding** is sometimes used to refer to exterior wall coverings made of wood, its meaning may be extended to include any type of finish covering on a frame building (with the exception of masonry). The term **cladding** is often used to describe any exterior wall covering, including masonry. Some common types of siding found on houses build before 1945 are listed below:

- **asbestos-cement siding.** A stiff cladding made of asbestos fiber and portland cement; most commonly seen as long shingles, often with a simulated wood grain surface; may be painted.

- **asphalt siding.** Made from saturated felts coated with asphalt and having mineral ("metal") granules on the side exposed to the weather; manufactured in shingle form, in rolls, or in panels with an insulated backing. Roll materials often have differently colored and embossed mineral surfaces that simulate brick and stone. A frequently seen example of this type of siding is

asphalt roll brick siding. It was a popular method of covering inferior or badly weathered wood cladding in the middle part of this century.

- **bevel siding, clapboard, lap siding**. This type of siding consists of boards that are thicker on one edge than the other; the bottom (thick) edge of one board overlaps the top (thin) edge of the board below.

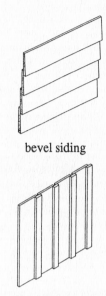

bevel siding

- **board and batten siding**. A siding consisting of long vertical boards and thin strips, or battens; the battens are used to conceal the gaps between the siding boards.

board and batten siding

- **drop siding, novelty siding, rustic siding**. A type of cladding characterized by overlapping boards with either tongued and grooved or rabbeted top and bottom edges. Oftentimes, the upper part of each board has a concave curve, in which case the siding is sometimes referred to as **German siding**.

drop siding

- **rabbeted bevel siding, weatherboarding**. A type of cladding characterized by beveled overlapping boards with rabbeted upper edges; a popular type of wood siding in early-American domestic architecture.

rabbeted bevel siding

- **shiplap, shiplap siding, shiplapping**. Siding where the top and bottom edges

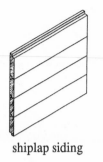

shiplap siding

sill plate

are dressed so as to make a close-fitting rabbeted or lapped joint.

sill

The framing member that forms the lower side of an opening, such as a **door sill**. A **window sill** forms the lower, usually projecting, lip on the outside face of a window. The term **lug sill** is sometimes used to describe a window sill that extends beyond the width of a window opening. A **slip sill** is a simple window sill (e.g., a stone slab or the like) that is only as wide as the window opening.

sill plate

The horizontal member that rests on the foundation and forms the lowest part of the frame of a structure.

Synonyms: **foundation plate, sill**

sleepers

Strips of wood laid over a concrete floor thereby providing a base to which flooring may be nailed or glued. Also, timbers, heavy beams, or logs laid on the ground to receive floor joists and help distribute the load. (This latter type of sleeper is most frequently found in cabin construction.)

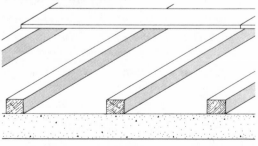

sleepers

sliding door
A door that slides on horizontally mounted tracks.

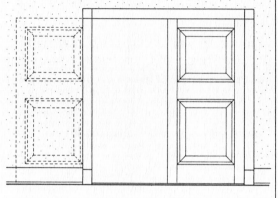

sliding door

sliding window
A window that moves horizontally in grooves, on strips, or between runners.
Synonyms: **sliding sash**

sliding window

smoke chamber
The transitional area between the throat of the fireplace and the bottom of the chimney flue. See illustration on page 76.

smoke shelf
A shelf in the smoke chamber used to redirect downdrafts back up the chimney flue. See illustration on page 76.

snow guard
Any device used to prevent snow from sliding off a sloped roof, or prevent snow from sliding down and clogging gutters. Snow

guards in the form of a loop of wire are often called **snow hooks**; ones in the form of small wooden rails, or cleats, are sometimes called **snow gratings**.

soffit
The exposed underside of an arch, cornice, balcony, beam, etc.; sometimes embellished with **soffit panels** or other decorative devices.

Southern Colonial (1600 - 1700)
An architectural style characterized by: one story or a story and a half, two end chimneys, brick (sometimes timber) construction, linear floor plan (i.e., one room deep), steeply pitched gable roof, and (sometimes) decorative treatment through the use of a variety of brick bonds and classical features (e.g., modillioned cornices, molded stringcourses, etc.).

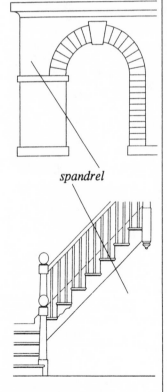

spandrel

spall
A fragment or chip removed from the face of a brick, stone, or other related material.

spandrel
The triangular space between the shoulder of an arch and the rectangular framework that surrounds it; the space between two adjacent arches; the triangular space between the outer string of a stair and the floor.

Spanish Colonial (1600 -1900)
An architectural style best known by the simple adobe to imposing Baroque inspired

missions of the Southwest. Domestic architecture characterized by: single story structures with flat or low pitched roofs, stucco covered stone or adobe brick walls, multiple doors, and sometimes verandas as well as courtyards (patios) with corridors (interior verandas).

spiral stair
A circular stair whose treads travel around, and are attached to, a central newel.
Synonyms: **spiral staircase, circular stair, corkscrew stair**

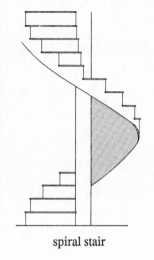

spiral stair

spline
A thin piece of wood or metal that is inserted into two joining members; found in joints with simple abutting members such as miters.
Synonyms: **feather, slip feather, slip tongue, false tongue**

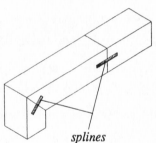

splines

spline joint
A term for any joint that incorporates a spline.

springer
The lowest voussoir of an arch; the flat or sloping stone that rests on the impost and from which the arch "springs;" the impost of an arch. Sometimes the term **skewback** is used to describe a sloping surface that serves as a support for the end of an arch. See illustration on page 72.

square notch
A corner notch formed by removing square blocks of wood from the top and bottom of a

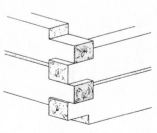

square notch

member. (Note its similarity to the double notch.)
Synonyms: **quarter notch**

stair
One step in a flight of stairs. For the parts of a stair see: nosing, riser, tread, winder.

staircase
A flight of stairs including handrails, newels, balustrades, landings, and strings.

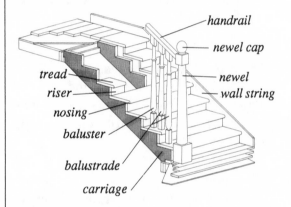

stair well, wellhole
A **stair well** is the vertical compartment that contains a staircase. A **wellhole** is the void, or clear space, between flights of stairs that are not in the same vertical plane (e.g., open newel and geometrical stairs have wellholes, whereas dogleg stairs do not).

stenciling
The process whereby a print, often polychromatic, is transferred to a wall or other surface by way of a brush and stencil.
Synonyms: **stencil work**

stickwork
A construction technique where major framing members, as well as more purely decorative members, are placed on top of the exterior siding; this exposed frame construction serves as the dominant design feature on Stick style houses.

stickwork

stile
A vertical member of a paneled door. The vertical section to which a lock is attached is called the **locking stile** or **shutting stile**; the vertical section to which the hinge is fastened is called the **hanging stile**. See illustration on page 133.

stilted arch
An arch whose curve begins above the level of the imposts.

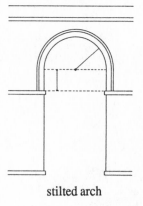

stilted arch

stone dressing
That part of stonework that involves surface preparation. The five traditional ways of dressing stone are: 1) hand or machine sawing, 2) rubbing with an abrasive, 3) hewing with an ax or pick, 4) hammering with an ax or hammer, and 5) chiseling with a mallet or hammer. Usually hard stone is hammer dressed and soft stone is hewn or chiseled. A representative sample of the numerous methods employed in dressing the face of squared stone follows:

- **broached.** A method of dressing stone with a pointed or narrow chisel so as to leave continuous parallel grooves;

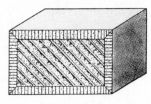

broached

grooves are usually diagonal, but may also be horizontal or vertical; used to finish sandstone and, less frequently, limestone.

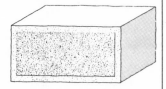

brush hammered

- **brush hammered.** A stone dressing method involving the use of a brush hammer (a hammer consisting of rows of pyramidal points). Through this technique a stipled surface is created; used on granite and hard limestone.

- **crandelled.** A stone dressing method involving the use of a crandall (a hammer-like tool with a number of pointed steel rods held in a slot at the end of a handle). A crandalled finish is a quick method of dressing principally sandstone; the finished surface usually has a fine, pebbly appearance.

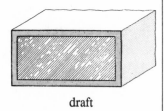

draft

- **draft, draft line, margin.** A narrow dressed strip along the edges of the face of a squared stone; usually cut with a chisel, but often cut with an ax or hammer in harder stone. Sometimes a draft serves only as a guide for removing the remainder of the face to a given level.

- **drove work, tooled work.** The final operation after tooth chiseling. After a soft stone is roughly dressed, the ridges left by tooth chiseling are removed by either a drove (a wide steel chisel measuring two to three inches in width) or a tool (a chisel measuring three and one-half to four and one-half inches in width). Usually the grooves made by the tooth chisel show to some extent after the surface has been drove or tool worked.

- **machined, machine worked.** Many surface finishes, such as droved, rubbed, polished, and grooved, could be accomplished by machine; usually cheaper than hand working when cutting and dressing large quantities of stone.

patent-hammered

- **patent-hammered.** A stone dressing method involving the use of a patent hammer (a two-headed hammer composed of from five to twelve thin parallel chisels). With each blow of the hammer several rows of short parallel grooves are made; generally used on granite and hard limestone.

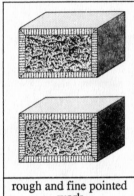

rough and fine pointed work

- **pointed work.** A stone dressing method characterized by either continuous or non-continuous shallow grooves made by a pointed tool. The term **rough pointed work** is sometimes used to describe surfaces with non-continuous grooves approximately one inch apart, and the term **fine pointed work** for surfaces with non-continuous grooves approximately one-half inch apart.

- **rock-faced, pitch-faced.** Ashlar or other stone whose face is given no additional finish except having its edges

rock-faced

rubbed finish

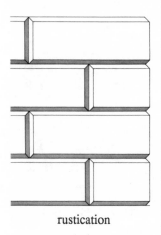

rustication

vermiculation

pitched off (cut true and in the same plane); may or may not have a well defined draft (border).

- **rubbed finish, polished finish.** A **rubbed finish** on sandstone and limestone is accomplished by hand or machine rubbing the surface of a stone until it is perfectly smooth. A **polished finish**, usually reserved for hard limestone, granite, and marble, involves machine or hand rubbing until a lustrous surface is obtained.

- **rustication, rusticated work.** Stone blocks separated from each other by deeply beveled or grooved joints.

- **tooth chiseled work.** The operation involving the preliminary reduction of soft stones through the use of a tooth chisel (a wide chisel with a serrated cutting edge). Tooth chisels are also used to dress drafts (borders).

- **vermiculation, vermiculated work.** A stone surface with deep grooves that resemble worm tracks.

stonework
Masonry construction in stone. The most common stones used in stonework are granite, gneiss, marble, porphyry, limestone, and sandstone.
Synonyms: **stone masonry**

stool
The casing or molded piece running along the base of a window and contacting the bottom rail on the inside of a building.
Synonyms: **window stool, window board, elbow board, stool casing**

stoop
An entrance platform, usually with several steps leading up to it; the term is sometimes used synonymously with **porch.**

stop
The vertical strip against which a window sash rests.
Synonyms: **window stop**

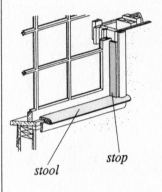

stool   *stop*

strapwork
A type of ornament resembling interlaced, or geometrically formed, studded leather bands; found on ceilings, screens, etc.

string
Also called **stringer** and **stringboard,** this term is used to describe the sloping side boards of a staircase supporting the ends of risers and treads. Sometimes the carriage supports the ends of risers and treads, and the string only serves as a cover for this rough work. This type of string is often referred to as a **finished string.** Strings may further be broken down into three types:

- **open string.** A string whose top edge is cut to the profile of the stairs so that treads project beyond the vertical plane

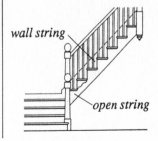

wall string

open string

of the string. Such a stair is called an **open stair** or **open string stair**.

closed string

- **closed string** (or **close string, housed string, curb string**). A string in which the ends of the treads and risers are received by grooves cut into the inner face of the string and are therefore concealed. Note that the top edge of the closed string is straight and parallel to the bottom edge.

- **wall string**. A string that rests against a wall or partition.

stringcourse

stringcourse
A continuous horizontal band of brick, stone, or wood on the exterior wall of a building; used for decorative purposes, or as a means of breaking up a large expanse of wall surface. When the purpose of a stringcourse is to shed rainwater (i.e., it consists of a continuous horizontal drip molding) it is often referred to as a **dripstone course**.
Synonyms: **belt course, sailing course, cordon**

structural clay tile

structural clay tile
A hollow cellular masonry unit composed of burnt clay, shale, or fireclay; made in a variety of forms and sizes; used for partitions and exterior walls (especially curtain walls). Synonyms: **hollow tile**

stucco
An exterior wall covering consisting of a mixture of portland cement, sand, lime, and

water; or a mixture of portland cement, sand, hair (or fiber), and sometimes crushed stone for texture; this term is often used synonymously with cement plaster.

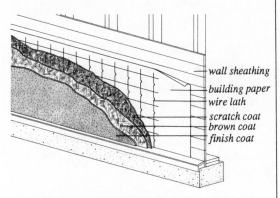

wall sheathing
building paper
wire lath
scratch coat
brown coat
finish coat

a typical stucco wall

studio
A room reserved for artistic pursuits.

studs
In wood frame structures, the slender vertical members used in wall and partition construction (typically 2x4s or 2x6s). See illustrations at right and on page 83.
Synonyms: **studding**

study
A retreat in a house used for reading, writing, and studying; frequently furnished with a desk, book shelves, etc.

subfloor
Rough boards or plywood sheets that are nailed directly to the floor joists and serve as a base for the finish flooring.

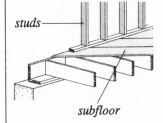

studs

subfloor

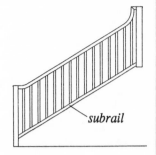

subrail

subrail
A molded member that is attached to the top edge of a closed string. The subrail acts as a receiving base for the balusters.
Synonyms: **shoe**

summer kitchen
An auxiliary kitchen, often added to a house at a later date; used when additional cooking or food preparation space is required, or when a particular household chore involves heat or mess that would more comfortably be carried out in a space more removed form the main living areas.

sunburst

sunburst
An ornamental motif resembling the rays of the sun; found most often on the facades of late-Victorian buildings.

swag
A festoon resembling a piece of cloth draped over two supports.

summer
In timber framing, a large beam that runs from girt to girt and carries one end of the floor joists. See illustration on page 168.
Synonyms: **summer tree, summer beam, dormant tree**

tenon
A projection, or tongue, on the end of a member. See illustration on page 111.

terra cotta

A fine-grained fired clay product used ornamentally on the exterior of buildings; may
be glazed or unglazed, molded or carved;
usually brownish red in color, but may also
be found in tints of gray, white, and bronze.

terrones

Blocks made of sun-baked river bottom sod;
used as a building material in older homes in
some parts of the Southwest. **Terron** is
generally stronger than adobe because it is
reinforced with roots and organic fibers.

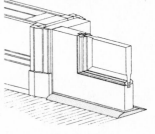

threshold

A wood or metal strip, or piece of stone, under
a door; used for weather protection or for
covering floor joints below the door.
Synonyms: **door saddle**

threshold

tie

Any structural member used to hold two parts
together.

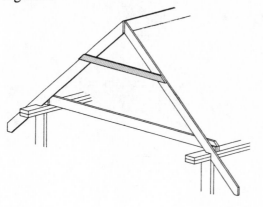

the collar beam shown above is an example of a tie

tie beam
A tie; a horizontal structural member connected to the feet of principal rafters of a truss to prevent them from spreading. See illustration on page 173.

tile
A piece of fired clay that is thinner than a brick.

timber framing
A framing system that uses timbers as structural elements; generally, the timbers range in size from 4x4s to 9x15s. Although timber framing is still used to a limited extent today — mostly for large outbuildings — it was in wide use until balloon framing was introduced in the early 1830s.
Synonyms: **timber frame construction**

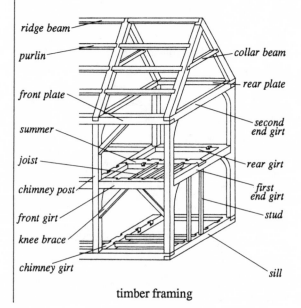

ridge beam
purlin
front plate
summer
joist
chimney post
front girt
knee brace
chimney girt
collar beam
rear plate
second end girt
rear girt
first end girt
stud
sill

timber framing

toe joint
A joint characterized by a horizontal member receiving another member at some acute angle.

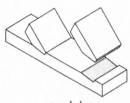
toe joint

toenailing
A means of securing two abutting members by driving of nails, spikes, or brads at an angle.

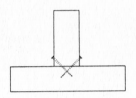
toenailing

tongue
The projecting rib along the edge of a member that fits into a corresponding groove in an adjacent member.

tongue and groove
A joint composed of a rib (tongue) received by a groove.

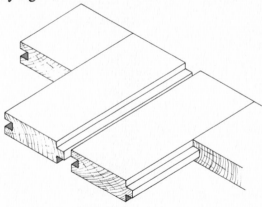
tongue and groove

tongue and lip joint
A type of tongue and groove joint that incorporates a flush bead on the side of the tongued member.

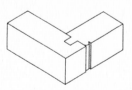
tongue and lip joint

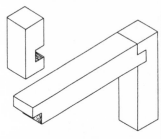

tongue and rabbet joint

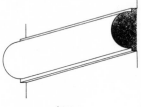

torus

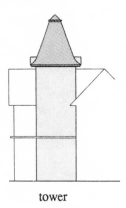

tower

tongue and rabbet
A joint formed when a tongued member is joined with a rabbeted member.

torus
A large convex molding of semicircular, or nearly semicircular, profile.

tower
A structure whose height is usually much greater than its width; may either stand alone or surmount a building.

T-plate
A T-shaped metal plate used for securing two perpendicular abutting members to one another.

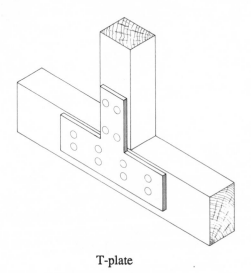

T-plate

tracery
The ornamental work in the upper part of an arched (Gothic) window consisting of inter-

lacing lines. Also, such decoration found on panels, screens, or rose windows (i.e., large circular windows, such as those found on church facades).

transom window

A small window or series of panes above a door, or above a casement or double hung window. The horizontal member that separates a transom window from the door or window below is called a **transom bar**, or **transom sill**.

Synonyms: **transom light, transom**

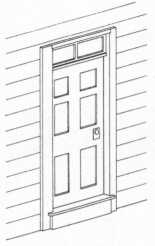

transom window above a cross and bible door

trapdoor

A door set into the surface of a floor or ceiling. Trapdoors are usually lifted or slid out of the way to allow access.

tread

The horizontal part of a stair step. See illustration on page 158.

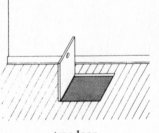

trapdoor

trellis

A latticework construction, such as a summerhouse. Also, a light frame or latticework used as a screen, or as a support for vines.

Synonyms: **treillage**

triglyphs

The group of three vertical bands found on the Doric frieze or its derivatives; alternates with the metopes. See illustration on page 15.

trim
The interior decorative finish around a door or window; the architrave or decorative casing used around a door or window frame. Synonyms: **door/window trim, inside casing**

trimmer
A doubled, or extra thick, joist or rafter placed on a side of a floor or roof opening and into which headers are framed.

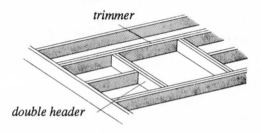

trimmer

double header

truss
A truss is essentially a triangle formed by any one of a combination of structural members into a rigid roof framework for spanning between two load-bearing walls. Generally, trusses are used when the span between two such walls exceeds 20 to 35 feet. Although there are numerous truss configurations (e.g., *Pratt truss*, *Fink truss*, *Howe truss*, *scissors truss*, etc.) the **king post truss** and the **queen post truss** are most often used in light construction. These two types, along with the names of their various structural components, are illustrated on the following page. The **gusseted W-type truss** is a type of truss that is widely used today.
Synonyms: **roof truss, simple truss, trussed rafter**

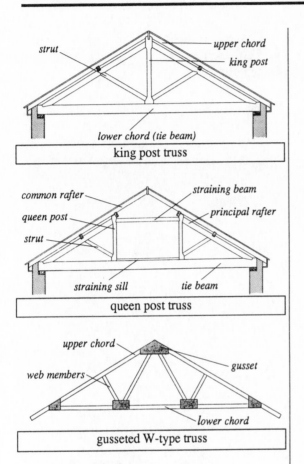

king post truss

queen post truss

gusseted W-type truss

Tudor (1890 - 1940)

An architectural style characterized by: steeply pitched end gabled roofs, gabled entryway, multi-paned narrow windows (usually in bands of three), tall chimneys (often with chimney pots), masonry construction, and decorative half-timbering in many cases.

turned wood ornament

An ornament made with a lathe; the resulting spindles are used as gable trim, as porch

turned wood ornament

friezes, etc. Sometimes referred to as **turned and chiseled work**.
Synonyms: **spindlework**

turret
A small and somewhat slender tower; often located at a corner of a building, in which case it is often referred to as a **corner turret**.

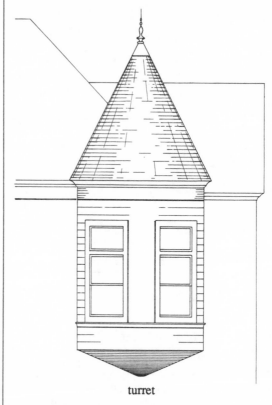

turret

Tuscan order
A classical order characterized by extreme simplicity: columns are not fluted; capitals are unadorned; and triglyphs — a characteristic feature of the Doric order — are absent.

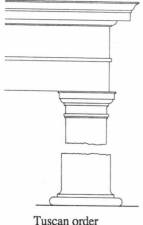

Tuscan order

tusk and tenon joint
A type of mortise and tenon joint characterized by the addition of a **tusk** (tooth) to the underside of the tenoned member.

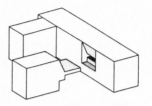

tusk and tenon joint

twisted column
A column that has a twisted or spiral appearance.
Synonyms: **wreathed column**

tympanum
The recessed triangular face of a pediment; sometimes contains a lunette, especially in domestic architecture.

tympanum

underpinning
The system of supports, such as rough walls or piers, beneath the ground floor. Also, the replacing or rebuilding of an infirm or old foundation so as to provide improved support.

valley
The depressed angle formed at the meeting point of two roof slopes.

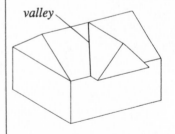

valley

vane
A metal ornament located atop a pinnacle, spire, or other elevated spot on a building; often rotates freely to indicate wind direction.
Synonyms: **weather vane**

vault
An arched ceiling or roof; an arched passageway. Unlike an arch, it has little more

than its own weight to carry. Three general classes of vaults are discussed below:

- **barrel vault, cylindrical vault, wagon** (or **waggon**) **vault, tunnel vault.** A continuous vaulted space with a semi-circular or pointed section.

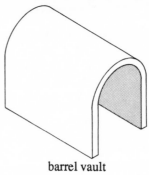

barrel vault

- **groined vault, groin vault, cross vault.** A vault formed by the intersection at right angles of two barrel vaults.

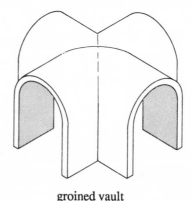

groined vault

dome

- **dome.** A vault that rests on a circular base and has a semicircular, segmental, pointed, or bulbous cross section.

vega
A projecting rounded roof beam found in pueblo style architecture of the Southwest. See illustration on page 43.

veneer
A decorative layer of brick, wood, or other material used to cover inferior structural material thereby giving an improved appearance at a low cost.

veranda
A roofed space attached to the exterior wall of a house and supported by columns, pillars, or posts; called **piazza** in earlier literature. A closely related term is **porch**, although its meaning usually is confined to a covered shelter over an exterior door.
Synonyms: **verandah**

vestibule
A small entrance room leading into a larger living space; a foyer; an anteroom.

vignette
A decorative motif characterized by scrolls adorned with grape clusters and leaves.
Synonyms: **vinette, trayle**

vignette

Vitruvian scroll
A series of scrolls connected so as to appear wave-like. See illustration on page 179.
Synonyms: **wave scroll, running dog, Vitruvian wave**

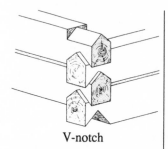

V-notch

V-notch
A corner notch formed when the tops of the joining ends of members are *pitched* (i.e., they have the appearance of an inverted "V").

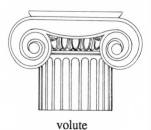

volute

volute
A spiralling scroll-like ornament. In classical architecture, the dominant feature of the Ionic capital (but also found on Corinthian and composite capitals as well).

voussoir
One of the wedge-shaped stones or one of the bricks, used in forming an arch. See illustration on page 72.

wallpaper
An interior wall covering of patterned paper. By the 1750s wallpaper had become a popular substitute for plastered and paneled walls.

wall sheathing
Boards, or other material, applied to the framing members and serving as a base for the finished siding.
Synonyms: **sheathing**

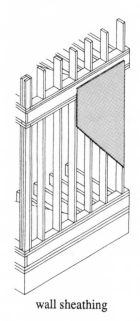

wall sheathing

wall ties
Metal strips of wire used to connect the two leaves of a cavity wall, or to firmly link facing to a backing. See **cavity wall** illustration on page 45.

water closet
A water-flushing device used to receive and discharge human waste. Also, a room containing a water closet.
Synonyms: **w.c.**

water leaf
An ornamental design element resembling a lotus or ivy leaf; used on molding.

water table
A plain or molded ledge or projection, usually at the first floor level, that protects the foundation from rain running down the wall of a building.

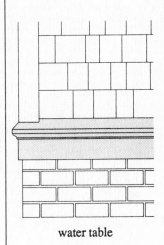

water table

wave molding
A molding that represents a series of breaking waves (i.e., one that incorporates a Vitruvian scroll).
Synonyms: **undulating molding, oundy molding, swelled chamfer**

wave molding

weather strip
A piece of wood, metal, or other material installed around window and door openings to prevent air infiltration and moisture penetration.
Synonyms: **weather stripping**

Western Stick (1890 - 1920)
An architectural style characterized by: a low pitched gable roof with widely overhanging eaves, roof rafters and purlins that extend well beyond the roof surface, beams (or joists) that extend beyond the wall surface,

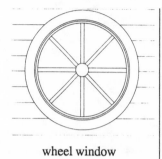

wheel window

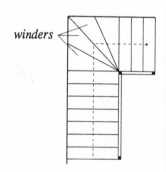

projecting balconies and porches, casement windows, and wood or shingle siding.

wheel window
A round window with glazing bars radiating from its center.

winder
A stair step with one end of the tread wider than the other end. Winders are used in spiral stairs and in stairs where steps are carried around curves or angles.
Synonyms: **wheel step**

winding stair
A stair constructed of winders; a stair that is carried around curves or angles.

window
A glazed opening in a wall that provides an interior space with natural light and ventilation. For descriptions of the parts of a window see: muntin, pane, parting strip, rail, sash, sill, stool, stop, and window frame.

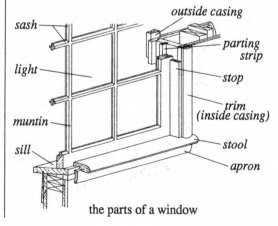

the parts of a window

window frame
The fixed frame of a window which is set in a wall to receive and hold the window and its associated hardware.

window guard
A protective, and often decorative, grille placed over a window.

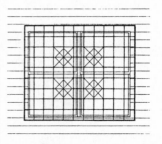

window guard

wing
A parallel extension to a building.

wood flooring
Hardwoods and softwoods in various sizes and configurations used for flooring. Four types of wood flooring are discussed below:

- **plank flooring, floorboards.** One of the oldest types of wood flooring, plank flooring originally consisted of long wide planks — these planks were often of random widths —fastened to the joists with wooded pegs. By the early-1800s, joints between floorboards were tongued and grooved, splined, butted, or shiplapped; at that time, pegging was largely replaced by face nailing and blind nailing (i.e., where nailing is done on the sides of the floorboards so as not to be visible). Plank flooring may be made of hardwoods (oak, maple, beech, birch, pecan, etc.) or softwoods (white pine, Norway pine, southern yellow pine, Douglas Fir, western larch, western hemlock, redwood, cypress, western red cedar, etc.).

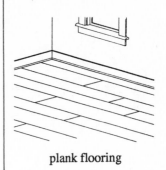

plank flooring

- **strip flooring, matched flooring, floorboards.** Plank flooring (discussed above) gradually evolved into long, narrow strip flooring. Generally, strip flooring is tongued and grooved along its sides and frequently along its ends as well (in which case it is often called **end-matched flooring**). Hardwood strip flooring is often found in more public living spaces; whereas softwood strip flooring is found in attics, closets, kitchens and the like, or is used as a base for resilient flooring (such as linoleum) or carpeting.

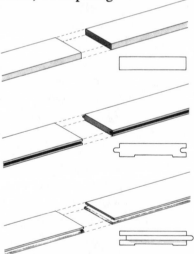

three examples of strip flooring

- **block flooring.** One type of block flooring, called **unit block** or **solid block flooring,** consists of strips of wood preassembled into square blocks; blocks may be either tongued and grooved or square ended and splined.

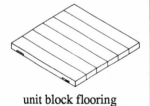

unit block flooring

Another type of block flooring, called **laminated block**, is made by bonding usually three layers of wood veneer together. Block flooring is available in a number of patterns that can be joined to simulate plank, strip, and parquet flooring. Woods such as cherry, teak, and walnut are often used with oak and maple to give a block floor more visual nterest.

laminated block flooring

- **parquet flooring.** A true parquet floor (versus a block floor with a parquet pattern) consists of short, narrow boards cut and joined to form various geometric patterns; usually at least two colors or two types of wood are used.

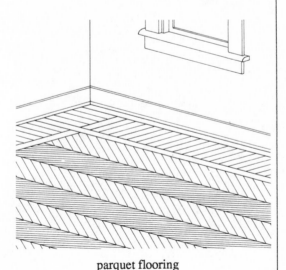

parquet flooring

wreath
An intertwined circular band or garland consisting of flowers, leaves, fruit, etc.

Cross References

This section contains the following headings:

- FRAMING
- ROOF AND ROOF TRIM
- STAIR
- WALLS
- FLOORS
- ARCHES
- COLUMNS AND CLASSICAL ELEMENTS
- WINDOWS
- FOUNDATIONS
- CEILINGS
- ROOMS / SPACES
- DECORATIVE ELEMENTS
- JOINERY
- FIREPLACE
- MASONRY
- DOORS
- STYLES (OF ARCHITECTURE)

Instructions:

Each of the above headings contains a list of all the main entries in the dictionary that pertain to that subject. To use the cross references, simply locate the heading that best fits the architectural element or feature you are trying to find. For instance, if the element is part of the skeleton or framework of a house, go to the **FRAMING** cross reference; if the element is purely ornamental in nature, go to the **DECORATIVE ELEMENTS** cross reference. Once at the most appropriate cross reference, search the list of entries until you find the term that fits.

FRAMING

balloon framing
beam
braced framing
brace
bridging
cantilever
collar beam
collar beam roof
cripple
doorframe
frame construction
framework
framing systems
girder
girt
gusset
half-timbering
hanger
head
header
heel
joists
ledger strip
lintel
lookouts

on center
planks
plates
platform framing
post
post bracket
post flare
purlins
rafters
rafter tail
ridge beam/board/pole
scantling
sill
sleepers
soffit
studs
summer
tie
tie team
timber framing
trimmer
truss
vega
window frame

belcast eaves
Boston hip
collar beam roof
compass roof
conical roof
corbelling
corbiestep
crest
curb roof
cut roof
eave
fascia board
finial
flashing
flat roof
gable roof
gambrel roof
gutter
hip
hip roof
hip and valley roof
hip gambrel roof
hip roll

imbrication
jerkinhead
lean-to roof
lookouts
louver
mansard roof
multiple roof
overhang
parapet
plancier
pyramidal hipped roof
ridge
ridge cap
roof covering
roofing tile
saltbox
sheathing
shed roof
snow guard
valley
vane
vergeboard

**ROOF AND
ROOF TRIM**

---

baluster
balustrade
banister
box stair
bracketed stair
carriage
dogleg stair
drop
easement
flier
flight of stairs
geometrical stair
handrail
handrail scroll
landing
newel
newel cap
nosing

open newel stair
ramp
riser
spandrel
spiral stair
stair
staircase
stair well
string
subrail
tread
winder
winding stair

STAIR

WALLS

anchor
apron
baseboard
base molding
base shoe
batten
battered wall
bearing wall
brackets
bull's eye
canale
cavity wall
chair rail
coping
corbel
corbel table
corbelling
corbiestep
corner boards
cornice
crenelation
curtain wall
curvilinear gable
cutaway corner
dado
downspout
facade
facing
foundation walls
frieze
furring
gable
gablet
gable trim
grille
gypsum lath

half-timbering
imbrication
lath
latticework
lunette
niche
outlet ventilator
overhang
panel
paneling
parapet
partition
pediment
plancier
plaster
plaster base
plinth
quoins
rainwater head
rake
raking molding
retaining wall
return
rustic work
screen
siding
stickwork
stringcourse
stucco
vega
veneer
wallpaper
wall sheathing
wall ties
water table

FLOORS

clay tile flooring
concrete flooring
encaustic
flagstone
flooring

grille
hatchway
resilient flooring
subfloor
wood flooring

abutment
arch
archivolt
compound arch
corbel arch
crown
elliptical arch
extrados
flat arch
haunch
impost
intrados
inverted arch
keystone
lancet arch
pier
pointed arch
relieving arch
segmental arch

soffit
spandrel
springer
stilted arch
vault
voussoir

ARCHES

abacus
apophyge
arcade
architrave
base
capital
colonette
colonnade
colossal column
column
composite order
Corinthian order
cornice
corona
coupled columns
cymatium
dado
dentils
Doric order
echinus
elephantine columns
engaged column

entablature
entasis
fascia
fluting
frieze
guttae
Ionic order
metope
modillions
mutules
neck
order
pedestal
pilaster
pillars
plinth
shaft
triglyphs
Tuscan order
twisted column
tympanum

**COLUMNS AND
CLASSICAL
ELEMENTS**

WINDOWS

apron
architrave
areaway
awning window
balconet
bay window
bow window
bull's eye
casement
casement window
casing
console
corner blocks
coupled windows
dormer
double hung window
drip
drip cap
embrasure
fanlight
fenestration
fixed sash
gablet
glass
glazing
hood
hopper window
lancet window
lattice window
leaded glass
leaf
lintel
lunette
mullion
muntin

oriel window
Palladian window
pane
parting strip
pediment
pivoted window
quarrel
Queen Anne sash
rail
reveal
sash
shutters
side light
sill
sliding window
stool
stop
transom window
trim
weather strip
wheel window
window
window frame
window guard

FOUNDATIONS

anchor bolts
backfill
draintile
footing
foundation
foundation walls

French drain
grade
mudsill
piers,pilings
underpinning

boss
ceiling
centerpiece
coffering
cove

crown molding
metal ceiling
panel
paneling
scuttle

CEILINGS

alcove
anteroom
ante-chamber
arcade
attic
balcony
basement
bathroom
bay
bedroom
borning room
buttery
cabinet
canopy
cellar
chamber
cistern
closet
conservatory
court
crawl space
cupboard
den
dependency
ell
entry
foyer
gallery
garderobe
garret
gazebo
hall
hall chamber
inglenook
keeping room
lantern

larder
lean-to
loft
nursery
outbuilding
outshot
pantry
parlor
parlor chamber
passageway
patio
pavilion
porch
porte-cochere
portico
stoop
studio
study
summer kitchen
tower
turret
veranda
vestibule
water closet
wing

ROOMS / SPACES

DECORATIVE ELEMENTS

acanthus
accessories
anthemion
Arabesque
astragal
ballflower
band
battled
bay leaf band
bead
bead and reel
bolection molding
cabling
cant molding
cartouche
cavetto
chamfer
channel
chevron
crenelation
cyma recta
cyma reversa
decorative half-timber-ing
denticulated
diaper
drop ornament
eclecticism
egg and dart
embellishment
festoon
figure
fillet
fleur-de-lis
flush bead
foliation
fret
garland
grotesque
guilloche
herringbone
hollow molding
hollow square molding

inlaid work
leaf
lozenge
lozenge molding
molding
mosaic
ornamental plasterwork
ornaments
ovolo
parquetry
patera
pearl molding
pendant
quirk
quirk bead
quirked molding
reeding
repoussé
reticulated molding
return bead
rinceau
roll molding
rosette
sawn wood ornament
scallop
scotia
scroll molding
scrollwork
shell
stenciling
strapwork
sunburst
swag
torus
tracery
turned wood ornament
vignette
Vitruvian scroll
volute
water leaf
wave molding
wreath

birdsmouth	mortise	
blocked	mortise and tenon	
bridle joint	notching	
butt joint	pin	
cogged joint	rabbet	
dado and rabbet	round notch	
diamond notch	saddle notch	
double notch	scab	
dovetail joint	scarf joint	
dovetail notch	semilunate notch	
doweling	shouldered housed joint	
finger joint	spline	**JOINERY**
fishplate	spline joint	
gain	square notch	
half notch	tenon	
haunch	toe joint	
heading joint	toenailing	
housed joint	tongue	
joinery	tongue and lip joint	
joint	tongue and groove	
kerfing	tongue and rabbet	
lap joint	T-plate	
lock Corner	tusk and tenon joint	
miter	V-notch	
miter joint		

ash dump	flue lining	
ash pit	hearth	
chimney	mantel	
chimney bar	mantelpiece	
chimney breast	mantelshelf	
chimney cap	overmantel	
chimney hood	panel	**FIREPLACE**
chimney pot	pediment	
chimney shaft	smoke chamber	
cricket	smoke shelf	
damper		
fireback		
fireboard		
fire frame		
fireplace		
flue		

MASONRY

adobes	jointing
arris	kiss marks
ashlar	masonry
ashlar masonry	masonry veneer
backing	mortar
brick	patterned brickwork
brick (surfaces)	pisé
brick (types)	pointing
brickwork	portland cement
brickwork (bonding)	riprap
brownstone	roughly squared
cement	rubblework
cement mortar	shale
concrete	spall
concrete block	stone dressing
concrete brick	stonework
face stones	structural clay tile
field stone	terra cotta
flagstone	terrones
galleting	tile

DOORS

architrave	hood
areaway	leaf
batten	lintel
batten doors	mullion
bulkhead doors	muntin
casing	panel
colonial panel door	paneled door
console	pediment
corner blocks	plinth block
door	rail
doorframe	reveal
door stop	screen door
Dutch door	scuttle
embrasure	side light
fenestration	sill
flush door	sliding door
French door	stile
glass	threshold
glazing	trapdoor
half-glass door	trim
hatchway	weather strip

New England Colonial (1600 - 1700)

Southern Colonial (1600 - 1700)

Spanish Colonial (1600 - 1900)

Dutch Colonial (1625 - 1830)

French Colonial (1700 - 1830)

Georgian (1700 - 1780)

Federal (1780 - 1830)

Greek Revival (1825 - 1860)

Gothic Revival (1830 - 1880)

Exotic Revivals (1835 - 1930)

Italianate (1840 - 1880)

Octagon (1850 - 1870)

Second Empire (1855 - 1890)

Eastern Stick (1860 - 1900)

Chateauesque (1860 - 1910)

Folk Victorian (1870 - 1915)

Colonial Revival (1870 - 1950)

Queen Anne (1880 - 1910)

Shingle (1880 - 1915)

Beaux Arts (1885 - 1925)

Western Stick (1890 - 1920)

Mission (1890 - 1920)

Richardsonian Romanesque (1880 - 1900)

Italian Renaissance (1890 - 1930)

Bungalow (1890 - 1940)

Tudor (1890 - 1940)

Prairie (1900 - 1920)

Neoclassical (1900 - 1940)

Pueblo Revival (1905 - present)

Art Deco (1920 - 1945)

International (1920 - 1945)

Art Moderne (1930 - 1945)

STYLES

Resources

DICTIONARIES AND ENCYCLOPEDIAS
(published after 1950)

Bianchina, Paul
  Illustrated Dictionary of Building Materials and Techniques. Blue Ridge Summit, PA: TAB Books, 1986.

Briggs, Martin Shaw
  Everyman's Concise Encyclopaedia of Architecture, with Line-drawings by the Author and 32 Pages of Photos. New York: Dutton, 1959.

Burke, Arthur E., J. Ralph Dalzell, and Gilbert Townsend
  Architectural and Building Trades Dictionary, Pearl Jenison, editor. Chicago: American Technical Society, 1950.

Cowan, Henry J.
  Encyclopedia of Building Technology. Englewood Cliffs, NJ: Prentice-Hall, 1988. (Consists of 210 short articles dealing with building technology; especially useful to the researcher are the lists of book and journal references at the end of each article.)

Fleming, John, Hugo Honour, and Nikolaus Pevsner
  The Penguin Dictionary of Architecture. New York: Penguin Books, 1966. (Sparsely illustrated, European orientation.)

Guedes, Pedro, editor
  Encyclopedia of Architectural Technology. New York: McGraw-Hill Book Company, 1979. (Contains a good section on building materials as well as other useful technical and stylistic information.)

Gwilt, Joseph
  The Encyclopedia of Architecture: Historical, Theoretical, and Practical, revised edition, originally published in 1867. New York: Crown Publishers, 1982.

Harris, Cyril M., editor
  Dictionary of Architecture and Construction. New York: McGraw-Hill Book Company, 1987. (Well illustrated and comprehensive.)

Hunt, William Dudly, Jr.
Encyclopedia of American Architecture. New York: McGraw-Hill, 1980.

Krieger, Morris
Homeowners' Encyclopedia of House Construction. New York: McGraw-Hill Book Company, 1978.

Putnam, R.E. and G.E. Carlson
Architectural and Building Trades Dictionary. New York: Van Nostrand Reinhold, 1983.

Saylor, Henry H.
Dictionary of Architecture. New York: John Wiley & Sons, 1963.

White, Norval
The Architecture Book. New York: Alfred A. Knopf, 1976.

Wilkes, Joseph A. and Robert T. Packard, editors
Encyclopedia of Architecture: Design, Engineering and Construction, Vol. 1. New York: John Wiley & Sons, 1987.

Yarwood, Doreen
Encyclopedia of Architecture. New York: Facts on File, 1986. (Comprehensive treatment of Western architecture; includes useful information on structural and ornamental elements, building materials, and architectural styles.)

DICTIONARIES AND ENCYCLOPEDIAS
(published before 1950)

Anonymous
The Builder's Dictionary: Or, Gentleman and Architect's Companion being a Complete Unabridged Reprint of the Earlier Work Published by A. Bettesworth and C. Hitch, 2 vols., originally published in 1734. Washington: Association for Preservation Technology, 1981. (This dictionary, Neve's *City and*

Country Purchaser, and Moxon's *Mechanick Exercises* are all very good sources for researching obscure or obsolete terms.)

Audsley, William J. and George A. Audsley
Popular Dictionary of Architecture and the Allied Arts: A Work of Reference for the Architect, Builder, Sculptor, Decorative Artist, and General Student, originally published in 1881. Woodbridge, CN: Research Publications, 1973.

Gwilt, Joseph
Encyclopedia of Architecture: Historical, Theoretical & Practical... London: Longmans, 1903.

Meikleham, Robert
Dictionary of Architecture... Philadelphia: A. Hart, 1851.

Neve, Richard
City and Country Purchaser and Builder's Dictionary, reprint of the 1726 edition. London: Thomas Kelley, 1969.

Nicholson, Peter
Encyclopedia of Architecture. A Dictionary of the Science and Practice of Architecture, Building, Carpentry... New York: Martin and Johnson, 1858.

Sturgis, Russell, editor
Dictionary of Architecture and Building: Biographical, Historical, and Descriptive. 3 vols, reprint of the 1902 edition. New York: Macmillan Company, 1901 - 1902. (The most comprehensive architectural dictionary written; its only disadvantage is that post-1900 terms are not covered. Reprinted in 1966 by Gale Research Co., Detroit, Michigan.)

GLOSSARIES AND PICTORIAL GUIDES

Binfield, Richard A.
Residential Architectural Styles. Chicago: Association of Real Estate Boards, 1953.

Blackburn, Graham
The Parts of a House. New York: Richard Marek Publishers, 1980.

Blumenson, John J.-G.
Identifying American Architecture: A Pictorial Guide to Styles and Terms, 1600-1945. Nashville: American Association for State and Local History, 1977. (Succinct and informative; gives brief description of American architectural styles as well as a pictorial glossary of the more common architectural terms.)

Brunskill, Ronald W.
Illustrated Handbook of Vernacular Architecture, 3rd ed. London: Faber & Faber, 1987. (Although the book deals with English vernacular architecture, it still contains much useful information.)

Devlin, Harry
What Kind of House Is That? New York: Parents' Magazine Press, 1969.

Foley, Mary Fix
The American House. New York: Harper & Row, Publishers, 1980. (A well illustrated and comprehensive chronology of American architectural styles; includes information on the European antecedents of American domestic architecture.)

Garnsey, George O.
The American Glossary of Architectural Terms... Chicago: The Clark and Langley Co., 1887.

Hammett, Ralph W.
Architecture in the U.S.: A Survey of Architectural Styles since 1776. New York: John Wiley & Sons, 1976.

Harris, John and Jill Lever
Illustrated Glossary of Architecture, 850-1830. New York: Clarkson N. Potter, 1966.

Isham, Norman Morrison
Early American Houses: and, A Glossary of Colonial Architectural Terms. New York: Da Capo Press, 1967.

Kauffman, Henry J.
The American Farmhouse. New York: Hawthorn Books, 1975. (Includes a section on outbuildings as well as numerous floor plans.)

King, A. Rowden
Realtors' Guide to Architecture: How to Identify and Sell Every Kind of Home. New York: Prentice-Hall, 1954.

Mansell, George
Anatomy of Architecture. New York: A & W Publishers, 1979.

McAlester, Virginia and Lee McAlester
A Field Guide to American Houses. New York: Alfred A. Knopf, 1986. (A comprehensive treatment of architectural styles and forms; organized by house types; has a nice visual glossary.)

McKee, Harley J.
Amateurs Guide to Terms Commonly used in Describing Historic Buildings, Following the Order Used by the Historic American Buildings Survey, Architect's Work Sheet for Photo-data Books. Rochester: The Landmark Society of Western New York, 1967.

Morrison, Hugh
Early American Architecture: From the First Colonial Settlement to the National Period. New York: Oxford University Press, 1952.

Parker, John Henry
Glossary of Architecture. Oxford: John Henry Parker, 1840.

A Concise Glossary of Terms Used in Grecian, Roman, Italian, and Gothic Architecture. reprinted from the 1894 edition. Wolfeboro, NH: Longwood Publishing Group, 1980.

Pitts, Carolyn
The Cape May Handbook. Philadelphia: The Atheneum of Philadelphia, 1977.

Poppeliers, John, S. A. Chambers, and N. B. Schwartz. *What Style Is It?* revised edition. Washington: Preservation Press, 1983.

Pothorn, Herbert
Architectural Styles. New York: Viking Press, 1971.

Rifkind, Carole
A Field Guide to American Architecture. New York: New American Library, 1980. (An excellent guide that uses building materials, plan, and elevation to describe the various styles; contains a very usable glossary.)

Rosengarten, Albert
A Handbook of Architectural Styles. New York: C. Scribner's Sons, 1901.

Sloane, Eric
An Age of Barns. New York: Ballentine Books, 1967. (Includes drawings of root cellars, ground cellars, spring houses, sugar houses, corncribs, tobacco barns, smokehouses, forge barn, milk house, cider house, washhouse, butchering shed, hop barn, wagon shed, outdoor oven, and icehouse.)

Walker, Lester
American Shelter: An Illustrated Encyclopedia of the American Home. Woodstock, NY: Overlook Press, 1981. (Chronologically presents the different types of dwellings found in America from the Southwestern Indian Pueblo to the Post Modern home; the numerous line drawings make this book a good choice for those who need a quick method of identifying styles.)

Washington State Historic Preservation Program
Architectural Description Guide. Olympia: Office of Archaeology and Historic Preservation, 1978.

Whiffen, Marcus
American Architecture Since 1780: A Guide to the Styles. Cambridge: M.I.T. Press, 1969. (A concise treatment of American architectural styles; describes the physical characteristics and history of each style.)

HISTORIC PRESERVATION AND RESTORATION

Anderson Notter Associates Inc.
The Salem Handbook: A Renovation Guide for Homeowners. Salem, MA: Historic Salem Inc., 1977.

Beckham, Stephen Dow
Identifying and Assessing Historical Cultural Resources in the Pacific Northwest. Portland, OR: U.S.D.A. Forest Service, 1978.

Bowyer, Jack, editor
Handbook of Building Crafts in Conservation: A Commentary on Peter Nicholson's The New Practical Builder and Workman's Companion, 1823. New York: Van Nostrand Reinhold Company, 1981. (Includes chapters on: brick-work, masonry, carpentry, joinery, plumber's leadwork, slating, glazing, plastering, and painting.)

Bullock, Orin M. Jr.
The Restoration Manual. Norwalk: Silvermine Publishers, Inc., 1966. (This book contains a glossary of architectural terms compiled by an English architect in 1853. It is worth noting, though, that many of these words are either obsolete or were never used in the United States.)

Dewitt, Susan V. and Jonathan M. Teague
The Old House Workbook: Rehabilitation Guidelines for Albuquerque. Albuquerque: Neighborhood Housing Services of Albuquerque, 1980. (Includes sections on researching the history of a house, principles of rehabilitation design, and rehabilitation guidelines.)

Falkner, Ann
Without Our Past: A Handbook for the Preservation of Canada's Architectural Heritage. Toronto: University of Toronto Press, 1976.

Hotton, Peter
So You Want to Fix Up an Old House. Boston: Little, Brown and Company, 1979.

Maddex, Diane, editor
All About Old Buildings: The Whole Preservation Catalog. Washington: The Preservation Press, 1985. (A must for the preservationist or the old house enthusiast; full of useful information including an extensive bibliography broken down by subject.)

McKee, Harley J.
Recording Historic Buildings. Washington: National Park Service, 1968.

McKenna, H. Dickson
A House in the City: A Guide to Buying and Renovating Old Row Houses. New York: Van Nostrand Reinhold, 1971.

New York State Board for Historic Preservation
Historic Resources Survey Manual. Albany: Division for Historic Preservation, Office of Parks and Recreation, 1972.

Oakland, City Planning Department
Rehab Right: How to Rehabilitate Your Oakland House without Sacrificing Architectural Assets. Oakland, 1978. (Contains descriptions and illustrations of 16 architectural styles and many useful drawings of features one might typically find in an older home.)

Office of Archaeology and Historic Preservation
Architectural Description Guide, Developed for Use in Preparing Nominations for State and National Registers of Historic Places. Olympia, WA., 1979. (Intended for those performing physical descriptions of historic buildings; contains short definitions and simple line drawings.)

Parker, Judith, and others, consulting editors
Living with Old Houses, 2nd revised edition. Portland, MN: The Advisory Service of Greater Portland Landmarks, 1975.

Rooney, William F.
Practical Guide to Home Restoration. New York: Bantam/Hudson Idea Books, 1980.

Stephen, George
Remodeling Old Homes without Destroying their Character. New York: Alfred A. Knopf, 1978.

U.S. Department of the Interior
The Secretary of the Interior's Standards for Historic Preservation Projects: with Guidelines for Applying the Standards. Washington: U.S. Department of the Interior, National Park Service, Preservation Assistance Division, 1985.

Webber, Joan
How Old is your House? A Guide to Research. Chester, CN: The Pequot Press, 1978.

BUILDING TECHNOLOGY
(books published after 1950)

Anderson, L.O.
How to Build a Wood-frame House. New York: Dover Publications, 1970. (Contains many clear illustrations relating to wood frame construction.)

Association for Preservation Technology
Association for Preservation Technology Bulletin, 2(1-2), 1970. (Special edition devoted to historic types of roofing.)

Barnes, Mark R.
"Adobe Bibliography." *Association for Preservation Technology Bulletin,* 7(1): 89-101, 1975.

Berkeley, Bernard
Floors: Selection and Maintenance. Chicago: American Library Association, 1968.

Blackburn, Graham J.
Illustrated Housebuilding. New York: Bonanza Books, 1978.

Brunskill, Ronald and Alec Clifton-Taylor
English Brickwork. London: Ward Lock Ltd, 1977.

Buchanan, Paul E.
"The Eighteenth-century Frame Houses of Tidewater Virginia." *Building Early America*, Charles E. Peterson, editor, pp. 54-73. Radnor, PA: Chilton Book Co, 1976.

Condit, Carl W.
American Building Art: The 19th Century. New York: Oxford University Press, 1960.

DiDonno, Lupe and Phyllis Sperling.
How to Design and Build Your Own House. New York: Alfred A. Knopf, 1978.

Elliott, Stuart and Eugenie Wallas
The Timber Framing Book. York, MN: Housesmiths Press, 1977. (Includes illustrations of joinery commonly used in timber framing as well as a glossary of terms.)

Frid, Tage
Tage Frid Teaches Woodworking. Joinery: Tools and Techniques. Newtown, CN: The Taunton Press, 1979.

Gillespie, Ann
"Early Development of the 'Artistic' Concrete Block: The Case of the Boyd Brothers." *Association for Preservation Technology Bulletin*, 11(2): 30-52, 1979.

Gilmore, Andrea M.
"Dating Architectural Moulding Profiles - A Study of Eighteenth and Nineteenth Century Moulding Plane Profiles in New England." *Association for Preservation Technology Bulletin*, 10(2): 91-117, 1978.

Harley, L.S.
"A Typology of Brick, with Numerical Coding of Brick Characteristics." *Journal of the British Archaeological Association*, 3rd series, 38: 63-87, 1974.

Harrison, Henry S.
Houses: The Illustrated Guide to Construction, Design and Systems. Chicago: National Institute of Real Estate Brokers of the National Association of Realtors, 1973.

Higgins, William J.
"Stone Finishing Marks." *Association for Preservation Technology Bulletin,* (11)3: 11-34, 1979.

Jordan, Terry G.
American Log Buildings, An Old World Heritage. Chapel Hill: University of North Carolina Press, 1985. (Excellent treatment of the subject; includes interesting information on Northern European precedents .)

Kauffman, Henry J.
The American Fireplace: Chimneys, Mantelpieces, Fireplaces and Accessories. New York: Thomas Nelson, 1972.

Loth, Calder
"Notes on the Evolution of Virginia Brickwork from the Seventeenth Century to the Late Nineteenth Century." *Association for Preservation Technology Bulletin,* 6(2): 82-120, 1974.

McKee, Harley J.
Introduction to Early American Masonry: Stone, Brick, Mortar and Plaster. Washington: National Trust for Historic Preservation, 1973.

Waite, Diana S.
"Roofing in Early America." *Building Early America.* Charles E. Paterson, editor, pp. 135-149. Radnor, PA: Chilton Book Co., 1976

BUILDING TECHNOLOGY
(books published before 1950, and reprints)

Benjamin, Asher
The Rudiments of Architecture: Being a Treatise on Practical Geometry, Grecian and Roman Mouldings, the Origin of Building, and the Five Orders of Architecture, reprint of 1814 edition. New York: De Capo Press, 1972.

Blake, Ernest G.
Roof Coverings: Their Manufacture and Application. London: Chapman & Hall, 1925.

Braley, E. Lindsay
Brickwork: A Comprehensive Treatise on the Theory and Practice of the Bricklayer, Including an Exposition of the Manufacture of the Customary Materials... London: Sir Isaac Pitman & Sons, 1947.

Carpenters' Co. of the City and County of Philadelphia
The Carpenters' Company 1786 Rule Book. Princeton, NJ: The Pyne Press, 1971.

Dietz, Albert G.
Dwelling House Construction, 2nd ed. New York: Van Nostrand Company, 1946.

Durbahn, Walter E.
Fundamentals of Carpentry, Volume I: Tools, Materials, Practice. Chicago: American Technical Society, 1949. (Contains an extensive glossary of carpentry terms.)

Graham, Frank D. and Thomas J. Emery
Audels Masons and Builders Guide #4. New York: Theo. Audel & Co., 1938. (A "how to" book for bricklayers, masons, and plasterers; contains illustrations of the tools, methods, and materials of these trades.)

Hodgson, Fred T.
Modern Carpentry. Chicago: Fredrick J. Drake and Co., 1903

Hooper, Charles Edward
The Country House: A Practical Manual of the Planning and Construction of the American Country Home and its Surroundings. New York: Doubleday, Page and Co., 1905.

Howe, Malverd A.
A Short Text-book on Masonry Construction, Including Descriptions of the Materials used, their Preparation and Arrangement in Structures, 1st edition. New York: John Wiley & Sons, 1915.

Huntington, Whitney Clark
Building Construction: Materials, and Types of Construction, 2nd edition. New York: John Wiley & Sons, 1941. (Excellent building construction sourcebook.)

International Correspondence Schools
International Library of Technology No. 30-B: Excavating, Shoring, and Piling, Footings and Foundations, Areas, Vaults, and Retaining Walls, Cements, Concrete Construction, Stone Masonry, Stone Arches, Carpentry, Joinery, the Steel Square. Scranton: International Textbook Company, 1909. (All of the International Library of Technology series have wonderful illustrations and informative text.)

International Library of Technology No. 31-B: Building Stone, Lathing, Plastering, and Tiling; Common Brickwork; Ornamental Brickwork and Terra Cotta; Lighting Fixtures; Use and Design of Lighting Fixtures; Architectural Design. Scranton: International Textbook Company, 1909.

International Library of Technology No. 33-B: Fireproofing of Buildings, Stair Building, Ornamental Metal Work, Builders' Hardware, Roofing, Sheet Metal Work, Mill Design. Scranton: International Textbook Company, 1909.

Masonry, Carpentry, Joinery: The Art of Architecture, Engineering and Construction in 1899. Chicago: Chicago Review Press, 1980. "Selections from the International Library of Technology published by the International Textbook Co., Scranton, Pa., beginning 1899."

Kidder, Frank E.
Building Construction and Superintendence. Part I. Mason's Work, 9th edition, revised. New York: William T. Comstock, 1909. (A very useful reference work; also very helpful in identifying architectural hardware.)

Lafever, Minard
The Modern Builder's Guide, reprint of the first (1833) edition with three additional plates from the third edition. New York: Dover Publications, 1969.

Langley, Batty
The Builder's Jewel: or, The Youth's Instructor and Workman's Remembrancer. Reprint of 1800 edition. New York: B. Blom, 1970.

Lowndes, William S.
Plastering and Stucco Work. Scranton: International Textbook Company, 1924.

Merrill, George F.
Stones for Building and Decoration, 3rd edition, revised. New York: J. Wiley & Sons, 1910.

Molloy, Edward, preparer
Roof Construction and Repair: Dealing with Slate, Tile, Asbestos-cement, Felt and Concrete Roofs, with a Special Chapter on Emergency Repairs. New York: Chemical Publishing Company, 1942.

Moxon, Joseph
Mechanick Exercises or the Doctrine of Handy-works, reprint of the 1703 edition. Scarsdale: The Early American Industries Association, 1975. (A fascinating look at 18th century carpentry and joinery techniques; includes plates showing the tools used by the various trades.)

Mulligan, John A.
Handbook of Brick Masonry Construction. New York: McGraw-Hill Book Company, 1942.

Newcomb, Rexford and William A Foster.
Home Architecture. New York: John Wiley & Sons, 1932.

Newlands, James
The Carpenter and Joiner's Assistant: Being a Comprehensive Treatise on the Selection, Preparation, and Strength of Materials, and the Mechanical Principles of Framing, With Their Application in Carpentry, Joinery, and Hand-railing. London: Blackie and Son, 1867. (Contains numerous finely executed etchings of construction details as well as an extensive glossary.)

Nicholson, Peter
The New Practical Builder and Workman's Companion....London: Thomas Kelly, 1823.

Price, C. Matlack
The Practical Book of Architecture. Philadelphia: J. B. Lippincott Co., 1916.

Seaton, Roy A.
Concrete Construction for Rural Communities, 2nd edition. New York: McGraw-Hill Book Company, 1918.

Townsend, Gilbert
Carpentry: A Practical Treatise on Simple Building Construction, Including Framing, Roof Construction, General Carpentry Work, Exterior and Interior Finish of Buildings, Building Forms and Working Drawings. Chicago: American Technical Society, 1949.

Townsend, Gilbert and J. Ralph Dalzell.
How to Plan a House. Chicago: American Technical Society, 1942.

ORNAMENTATION / DECORATIVE ARTS (books published after 1950)

Bridgeman, Harriet and Elizabeth Drury, editors
The Encyclopedia of Victoriana. New York: Macmillan Publishing Co., 1975. (Includes textile and wallpaper glossaries.)

Chapman, Suzanne E.
Early American Design Motifs. New York: Dover Publications, 1974.

Flaherty, Carolyn
"Sawn Wood Ornament." *The Old-house Journal Compendium*, Clem Labine and Carolyn Flarherty, editors, pp. 241-243. Woodstock, NY: Overlook Press, 1980.

Hamlin, A. D. F.
A History of Ornament. New York: Cooper Square Publishers, 1973.

Katzenbach, Lois and William Katzenbauch
Practical Book of American Wallpaper. Philadelphia: Lippincott, 1951.

Kettell, Russell Hawes, editor
Early American Rooms, 1650-1858. New York: Dover Publications, 1967.

Library of Victorian Culture
Late Victorian Architectural Details: An Abridged Facsimile of Combined Book of Sash, Doors, Blinds, Moulding, Stair Work, Mantels, and All Kinds of Interior and Exterior Finish. Watkins Glen, NY: American Life Foundation Study Institute, 1978.

Little, Nina Fletcher
American Decorative Wall Painting 1700 - 1850. New York: E. P. Dutton & Co., 1972.

Southworth, Suzan and Michael Southworth
Ornamental Ironwork: An illustrated Guide to its Design, History and Use in American Architecture. Boston: David R. Godine, Publisher, 1978.

Summerson, John
The Classical Language of Architecture. Cambridge: M.I.T. Press, 1963.

Van Dommelen, David B.
Walls: Enrichment and Ornamentation. New York: Funk & Wagnalls, 1965.

Wharton, Edith and Ogden Codman Jr.
The Decoration of Houses. New York: W. W. Norton & Co., 1978.

Weil, Martin Eli
"Interior Details in Eighteenth Century Architectural Books". *Association for Preservation Technology Bulletin,* 10(4): 47-66, 1978.

Wilson, H. Weber
"Window Glass." Old-house Journal, 6(4): 37+, 1978.

"Etched and Brilliant Cut Glass." *Old-house Journal,* 6(7): 77-78, 1978.

"Fancy Bevelled Glass." *Old-house Journal,* 6(11): 123-124, 1978.

ORNAMENTATION / DECORATIVE ARTS
(books published before 1950, and reprints)

Audsley, William James
Outlines of Ornament... New York: Scribner and Welford, 1882.

Clifford, Chandler R.
Period Decoration. New York: Clifford & Lawton, 1901.

Day, Lewis Foreman
The Application of Ornament. Reprint of 1888 edition. New York: Garland Publishing, 1977.

Halstead, Frank
Architectural Details. New York: John Wiley & Sons, 1927.

Lienard, Michel
Specimens of the Decoration and Ornamentation of the XIX Century... Boston: James R. Osgood and Co., 1875.

Meyer, Franz Sales
Meyer's Handbook of Ornament, Geometrical and Floral. Pelham, NY: Bridgman Publishers, 1928.

Pergolesi, Michelangelo
Classical Ornament of the Eighteenth Century. Originally published in 1777. New York: Dover Publications, Inc.

Speltz, Alexander
Styles of Ornament, Exhibited in Designs and Arranged in Historical Order with Descriptive Text... Chicago: Regan Publications, 1928.

Ware, William Robert
The American Vignola: A Guide to the Making of Classical Architecture. New York: Norton. Part I is based on the fourth edition of 1905 and Part II is based on the first edition of 1906, International Textbook Co. of Scranton, 1977.

PATTERN BOOKS AND RELATED WORKS

Bicknell, Amos Jackson
Bicknell's Village Builder: A Victorian Architectural Guidebook. Originally published in 1870. Watkins Glenn, NY: The American Life Foundation & Study Institute, 1976.

Bicknell, Amos J. and William T. Comstock
Victorian Architecture: Two Pattern Books... Watkins Glenn, NY: The American Life Foundation & Study Group, 1976.

Bruce's (George) Son and Company
Victorian Frames, Borders, and Cuts for the 1882 Type Catalog of George Bruce's Son and Co. New York: Dover Publications, 1976.

Bullock, John
*The American Cottage Builder: A Series of Designs, Plans, and Specifications from $200 to $20,000...*New York: Stringer and Townsend, 1854.

Cummings, Marcus Fayette and Charles Miller
Victorian Architectural Details: Two Pattern Books... Watkins Glen, NY: The American Life Foundation & Study Group, 1978.

Downing, A.J.
Cottage Residences: Or, A Series of Designs for Rural Cottages and Cottage-villas and their Gardens and Grounds. New York: Wiley and Putnam, 1842.

The Architecture of Country Houses. New York: D. Appleton, 1850.

Grow, Lawrence, compiler
Old House Plans: Two Centuries of American Domestic Architecture. New York: Universe Books, 1978.

Lakey, Charles D.
*Lakey's Village and Country Houses: Or, Cheap Homes for All Classes...*New York: American Builder Publishing Co., 1875.

Mason, Bernard S. and Frederick H. Kock
Cabins, Cottages, and Summer Homes. New York: A.S. Barnes & Company, 1960.

Newsom, Samuel and Joseph C. Newsom
Picturesque California Homes: A Volume of Forty Plates, Plans, Details and Specifications of Houses Costing from $700 to $15,000, and Adapted to Families Having Good Taste and Moderate Means. Reprint of 1884 edition. Los Angeles: Hennessey & Ingalls, 1978.

Palliser, George and Charles Palliser
The Palliser's Late-Victorian Architecture, a facsimile of George and Charles Palliser's *Model Homes* (1878) and *American Cottage Homes* (1878), and republished in 1888 under the title *American Architecture,and New Cottage Homes and Details* (1887). Watkins Glen, NY: The American Life Foundation & Study Institute, 1978.

Sloan, Samuel
*City and Suburban Architecture: Containing Numerous Designs and Details for Public Edifices, Private Residences, and Mercantile Buildings...*Philadelphia: J. B. Lippincott, 1859.

The Athenaeum Library of Nineteenth Century America
Two Pattern Books by A.J. Bichnell and William T. Comstock. Watkins Glenn, NY: The American Life Foundation & Study Institute, 1976.

Victorian Architectural Details: Two Pattern Books by Marcus Fayette Cummings and Charles Crosby Miller. Watkins Glen, NY: The American Life Foundation & Study Institute, 1978.

Vaux, Calvert
Villas and Cottages: A Series of Designs Prepared for Execution in the United States. Originally published in 1864 by Harper & Brothers, Publishers. New York: Dover Publications, 1970.

Woodward, George Evertson
Woodward's National Architect: Containing 1000 Original Designs, Plans and Details... New York: Geo. E. Woodward, 1868.

Index

A

abacus *15*
abutment *15*
acanthus *15*
accessories *16*
Adam *73*
adobe bricks *16*
adobes *16*
alcove *16*
American bond *37*
American common bond *37*
anchor *16*
anchor bolts *16*
angle posts *113*
ante-chamber *16*
anteroom *17*
anthemion *17*
anti-chamber *16*
apophyge *17*
apron *17*
Arabesque *17*
arbor *30*
arcade *17*
arcaded corbel table *55*
arch *17*
arch bricks *35*
architrave *18*
archivolt *18*
areaway *18*
arris *18*
Art Deco *18*
Art Moderne *19*
artistic concrete block *53*
asbestos shingles *138*
asbestos-cement siding *152*
ash dump *19*
ash pit *20*
ashlar *19*
ashlar masonry *19*
broken range work *19*
coursed range work *20*
random range work *20*
ashlar veneer *109*
ashler *19*
asphalt prepared roofing *141*
asphalt roll brick siding *152*
asphalt shingles *139*
asphalt siding *152*
asphalt tile *135*
astragal 21, *27*
attic *21*
awning window *21*

B

backfill *21*
backing *21*
bagnette 21, 27
baguette 21, 27
balconet 22
balcony 22
ball and flower 22
ballflower 22
balloon framing 22
baluster *23*
balustrade *23*
band *24*
banded column *24*
banister *24*
bar *112*
bargeboard *24*
barrel vault *176*
base 25, 51, 121
base cap *25*
base molding *25*
base shoe *25*
base shoe molding *26*
baseboard *25*
baseboard shoe *26*
basement *25*
basket weave *37*
bathroom *26*
bats *33*
batten *26*
batten door *26*
battered wall *26*
battled *27*
bay *27*
bay leaf band *27*
bay leaf garland *27*
bay window *27*
bead 21, 27
bead and quirk *130*
bead and reel *27*
bead joint *102*
bead molding *27*
beaded joint *102*
beading *121*
beam *27*
bearer *106*
bearing partitions *119*
bearing wall *28*
Beaux Arts *28*
bed (of a brick) *32*
bedroom *28*
belcast eaves *28*
belcast gambrel roof *28*

C

Words of Praise for
Old-House Dictionary

"Just the thing for anyone contemplating buying or restoring an old house. This charming, simply written reference source provides an illustrated guide to American domestic architecture from 1600 to 1940."
— *Library Journal*

"A fine dictionary of architectural terms for both beginners and professionals...It's all here. The drawings are exhaustively clear...lucid definitions...A proud book."
— *The Book Reader*

"...the 750-plus definitions presented in this attractive little volume are admirably concise and clear, often illustrated with uncommonly sharp drawings. "
— *American Reference Books Annual 1990*
Vol. 21, Libraries Unlimited, Inc.

"Straightforward in presentation...should prove to be a much-used reference source."
— *Reference Books Bulletin*

"...should prove to be of great value to people who own historic houses or are involved with the preservation and restoration of historic properties."
— *Peter D. Shaver, Newsletter Editor*
Preservation League of NY State

"This is no casual overview...[it] will be referred to by architects...students... general-interest owners..."
— *The Midwest Book Review*

"The clarity and precision of diction in the definitions is strengthened by the clarity and precision of the 450 line drawings..."
— *Wilson Library Bulletin*

"A fine addition to architectural literature."
— *Sanford Fish, Editor*
Preservation New Mexico